Amazed

30 DAYS OF GROWING IN AWE OF GOD

"The devotions in *Amazed* pack God-sized theology into digestible daily doses. By offering Christ-centered devotional thoughts in a conversational tone, Carolyn Lacey invites us to stand in awe of God through peering at some of his attributes. The beautiful format mirrors the beautiful prose!"

AIMEE JOSEPH, *Bible Teacher; Author, Look, Listen, Live: Cultivating Attention in a Distracted Culture*

"The more I study God's true character, the more I realize how much there is to learn—and I want more! That's why I'm so thankful for Carolyn Lacey's new book. In *Amazed,* she does a wonderful job of both exploring God's attributes through Scripture and leading readers to respond to the Lord in faith. I highly recommend this devotional!"

KATIE FARIS, *Author, Every Hour I Need You: 30 Meditations for Moms on the Character of God*

"I always appreciate Carolyn's writing and, with characteristic depth and clarity, Carolyn has given us a gift in these devotions as she gently invites us to slow down and take stock of how glorious our God is, and how worthy he is of our awe. Wonderfully though, she doesn't stop there. Grounded in the contours of everyday life, this is a winsome invitation that will stir you both to awe and prayerful action, as she leads you to consider how growing in your knowledge of the truth then leads to godliness."

SARAH DARGUE, *Co-Host, Two Sisters and a Cup of Tea podcast*

"Carolyn has collected well-known Bible verses and woven them together in a fresh way to lift our eyes from ourselves to see the greatness of our God. Wholesome, hope-filled and helpful, this book is a great gift to us and will make a great gift for others."

LINDA ALLCOCK, *Author, Deeper Still; Ministry Leader, The Globe Church, London*

"I love these God-centred meditations from Carolyn. She writes beautifully, with theological depth, and handles the narrative of Scripture skilfully. You will find in her a real kindred spirit, as she feeds your soul with the glories of our triune God. Moving you to worship with wonder and love and awe."

NATALIE BRAND, *Bible Teacher; Author, Priscilla, Where Are You? A Call to Joyful Theology*

"Humbling and awe-inspiring. Carolyn Lacey captures the wonder and lovingkindness of God—reminding us that he is both mighty and merciful."

JUSTINE ORDWAY, *Host, Going Deeper podcast*

Amazed

30 DAYS OF GROWING IN AWE OF GOD

CAROLYN LACEY

Amazed
30 Days of Growing in Awe of God

Published by:
The Good Book Company

thegoodbook.com | thegoodbook.co.uk
thegoodbook.com.au | thegoodbook.co.nz

Design by André Parker | Original series design by Jennifer Phelps

ISBN: 9781802543490 | JOB-008434 | Printed in India

For Tiana

May you gaze on the beauty of the Lord all the days of your life.

May you delight in all his perfections.

May you seek his face always.

Contents

His Glory

GAZING AT GOD'S HOLINESS

1

Longing for More

"The LORD, the LORD, the compassionate and gracious God, slow to anger, abounding in love and faithfulness, maintaining love to thousands, and forgiving wickedness, rebellion and sin."

EXODUS 34:6-7

Read Exodus 33:12-23

What are the sights, sounds, tastes and experiences that have left you longing for more?

As a child, I can remember the exhilarating swoosh of the playground swing as it carried me up into the sky. I kept on asking for more pushes so I could swing higher than I'd dared to fly before. A brave 4-year-old, I was no longer afraid of falling—I just wanted *more*.

Is this how you feel about the Lord? When it comes to knowing him, I know I'm barely scratching the surface, but I've found that the more I do know, the more amazed I am—and the more I want to know. Not just to satisfy my intellectual curiosity, but because greater knowledge of him leads to greater awe—and being in awe of God changes everything.

It's when our hearts are amazed by him that everything else is put into its rightful place. We don't feel the need to seek satisfaction and peace in people or experiences that can never measure up—we find them in him. We are freed from needless anxiety, endless comparison and misdirected worship. We stop pursuing our own glory—and learn to delight in his.

In Exodus 33, Moses makes a bold request of the Lord:

Show me your glory. (v 18)

I read those words hundreds of times before the thought struck me—*hasn't Moses already experienced God's glory?*

This episode in the ancient prophet's life follows his surprise encounter with the burning bush, his front-row seat to the miraculous signs performed in Egypt, his safe deliverance through the middle of the Red Sea, and his intimate conversations with the Lord in the tent of meeting, enshrouded by a pillar of cloud—not to mention the terrifying experience of the presence of the Lord as he descended on Mount Sinai, accompanied by thunder, lightning, smoke, fire and the sound of a trumpet! Moses has already seen so much of God's glory, but the cry of his heart is for more.

You see, glimpses of glory are not enough. God's glory is an unstoppable fountain of delight—an ocean of wonder whose depths cannot be sufficiently plumbed. Moses has tasted this glory, and he is left longing for more.

But God does not respond to Moses' request as he might expect. Moses cannot bear a full unveiling of the radiance and splendour of the Holy One—he (and any other human) cannot see God's face and live (v 20). But God will reveal more of himself to Moses through the proclamation of his name and character. He places Moses in the cleft of a rock and covers him with his hand until he has passed by. He shields him from glory he cannot bear, and graciously unveils his inner self—his heart for the people he calls his own:

> *The Lord, the Lord, the compassionate and gracious God, slow to anger, abounding in love and faithfulness, maintaining love to thousands, and forgiving wickedness, rebellion and sin. (34:6-7)*

It's as though he's saying to Moses, *If you want to see me, if you want to really know me, understand this: I am full of compassion, grace and patience. I am eternally loving, ever-faithful, brimming with mercy and forgiveness.*

When Moses prays, "Show me your glory", he is asking, *Show me who you are.* Before he continues to the Promised Land (with people who are sinful, rebellious and faithless) he needs to know more of the one who promises to go with him.

Maybe you feel like that too. If you are to continue trusting the Lord to lead you through the twists and turns of this life and safely through death into eternity with him, you want to know more of who he is. You need to know that you really can trust him.

Perhaps, like me, you read Old Testament accounts of God's glory being revealed, and long to witness these awe-inspiring sights and sounds yourself. God's answer to Moses shows that what we most need is a revelation of God's being, his nature, his heart. Like Moses, we could not cope with witnessing the fullness of God's glory. But in his kindness, he has wrapped his glory into human form in the Lord Jesus—so that we may know him intimately. The brightest reflection of God's glory is seen in the gospel of Jesus Christ:

> *For God, who said, 'Let light shine out of darkness,' made his light shine in our hearts to give us the light of the knowledge of God's glory displayed in the face of Christ.*
> *(2 Corinthians 4:6)*

We can look at Jesus—his perfect life, his sacrificial love, his triumph over death—and know that we are seeing *God himself.* Like Moses, we can ask God to show us even more of his glory. And we can be confident that, though it may look different than we anticipate, he *will* answer.

Cultivate

Consider how you have experienced glimpses of God's glory in your own life. Have these experiences left you longing for more, or have you begun to forget the wonder of compassion and grace, mercy and forgiveness towards sinners? Like Moses, don't be content with what you already know of the Lord; boldly ask for more.

Pray

Write your own prayer asking the Lord to reveal more of his character to you as you read his word, contemplate his works and spend time with his people. Pray it regularly throughout this 30 days of growing in awe, and note any specific ways in which the Lord answers you.

2

Glimpses of Glory

"Holy, holy, holy is the LORD *Almighty;*
the whole earth is full of his glory."

ISAIAH 6:3

Have you ever thought about what it is that makes God … *God?*

Perhaps you've pondered this kind of question a lot or maybe you think the answer is obvious: *he just is!*

We sometimes forget quite how different God is to you and me. Often, what we think about him is more likely to be based on our experience than on what he reveals about himself in his word and in our world. That's why I wanted us to first focus on God's glory—the display of his nature that reveals his total "otherness" or "God-ness". In other words, what it is that makes him God.

The prophet Isaiah was an ordinary human being like you and me. But he was given an extraordinary vision of God's glory.

Read Isaiah 6:1-5

> *I saw the Lord, high and exalted, seated on a throne; and the train of his robe filled the temple. (v 1)*

Judah's king, Uzziah, has died, verse 1 tells us; but the Lord is very much alive. He is immortal—reigning high on his throne, exalted above the earth and heavens.

Centuries earlier, God had told Moses, "No one may see me and live" (Exodus 33:20). And that is still true—Isaiah cannot see God's face (or even his back or his feet). All he sees is the hem of his garment *filling* the temple.

As a little girl, I remember watching the wedding of Charles and Diana, Prince and Princess of Wales, and being mesmerised by Diana's dress with its 25-foot train trailing behind her as she walked up the aisle of St Paul's Cathedral. But imagine the train of God's robe alone filling the magnificent temple Solomon had built 200 years earlier. If just the hem of his robe is too great to envisage, how glorious the Lord himself must be!

It's not only Isaiah who cannot look at this glorious God. The seraphim who attend him hide their faces, shielding their eyes from glory too great to behold. Seraphim means "burning ones"—these are not humans; they are heavenly creatures who stand in God's presence and serve him. The unveiled glory of God is so breathtakingly bright that no created being can gaze on it and remain standing—not even angelic beings who we might think would be used to it!

The seraphim call to one another:

> *Holy, holy, holy is the* Lord *Almighty;*
> *the whole earth is full of his glory. (Isaiah 6:3)*

There's a link here between God's holiness and God's glory. God's holiness is more than his moral purity—it's what sets him apart from every other creature. His holiness is his uniqueness; his divine essence; his supreme power, matchless beauty and absolute perfection; his incomprehensible and incomparable worth.

God cannot be compared to anyone or anything because he is in a class of his own—there is none like him (Isaiah 40:25; 1 Samuel 2:2; Hosea 11:9). And his glory is the outward display of his holiness—the revelation of who he really is. When God showcases his holiness, we see his glory.

As the seraphim proclaim God's holiness, the foundations of the doorways shake and the temple is filled with smoke. How petrifying this would be! For Isaiah, this is not a warm worship experience but a feeling of intense terror. God's glory is overwhelming, overpowering, awesome.

Isaiah falls on his face, undone. He realises he's in the presence of supreme holiness, and he is intensely conscious of his sin. A holy God inspires holy fear.

This must be our response too. As we glimpse true glory, we should be humbled and bow in reverent fear. His holiness exposes our sinfulness. The splendour of his glory exposes the hollowness of all the other things we trust in. But we don't need to stay on our faces, because the vision of his majestic glory also inspires deeper trust in his goodness and greater hope in his mercy. So we can lift our heads, our hands and our voices in joyful praise.

As we become more and more amazed by our gloriously holy God, we cannot help but worship.

Cultivate

Spend a few minutes contemplating God's holiness. How might a growing appreciation of his "otherness" impact your day-to-day life?

Listen to the song "Nothing Left to Say" by Davy Flowers.

Pray

Lord God, you are holy, holy, holy—the earth is full of your glory. As I glimpse your glory, I am aware of my smallness. As I contemplate your holiness, I am aware of my sinfulness. How amazing it is that one so magnificent cares about someone so insignificant. I am in awe of your perfection. I am humbled by your desire to be known by sinful people. Teach me to raise my voice and join the angels in praising and adoring you, because you alone are worthy. You alone are holy. Amen.

3

Indescribable Beauty

"High above on the throne was a figure like that of a man … Like the appearance of a rainbow in the clouds on a rainy day, so was the radiance around him. This was the appearance of the likeness of the glory of the Lord. *When I saw it, I fell face down."*

EZEKIEL 1:26-28

There's something about a rainbow that stops me in my tracks. No matter how familiar the sight, I still gasp with delight at the sight of a jewel-coloured arc beaming through a rainy sky.

The 16th-century theologian John Calvin once said:

There is no colour in this world that is not intended to make men rejoice.

If that is true (and I think it is!), a rainbow does its job exceptionally well! But it isn't just the beautiful colours shimmering amid raindrops that charm me. As I gaze at hazy yet distinct rings of red and gold, green and violet, the dark clouds seem less prominent and a promise of incoming brightness lifts my spirit.

Perhaps you feel the same. Rainbows are not simply a physical wonder to enjoy in the moment; they rekindle our longing for greater joys to come. So it seems fitting that in describing the radiant glory he sees surrounding the Lord, the prophet Ezekiel uses rainbow-language.

Read Ezekiel 1:22-28

God's people have been banished from their land because of their sin. Only the very poor are left in Judah; everyone else has been captured by the Babylonians and taken into captivity. While they are in exile by the Babylonian River Kebar, Ezekiel sees a spectacular vision of the glory of God. It starts with a storm cloud, flashing with lightning and fire. In the centre of the fire something gleams like amber, and as the cloud approaches, Ezekiel sees living creatures—like humans but with bronze legs, hooved feet and wings. He later realises they are cherubim (Ezekiel 10:1). Above the cherubim is a sparkling expanse of sky, glittering like crystal. And above this expanse is a throne of lapis lazuli occupied by a man-like figure of fire and metal.

Ezekiel sees the glory that Moses and Isaiah saw, but in a more up-close and personal way. He experiences more than fire and lightning, and he sees more than the hem of the Lord's garment. Ezekiel is given a glimpse into God's throne room as the heavens are opened (v 1). He sees through the shimmering expanse separating earth and heaven, beyond the startling blue throne, to the image of the one seated there.

It is a breathtaking scene and totally transcendent. Ezekiel is able to describe everything below the expanse—he offers vivid depictions of the creatures and directional details about the wheels accompanying them. But when he tries to convey what is above the expanse, his words falter. "What looked like … like that of … what appeared to be … as if

... like the appearance of" is the best he can offer, because it is not possible to describe the indescribable. He even hesitates to declare that he has seen the glory of the Lord, more tentatively suggesting, "This was the appearance of the likeness of the glory of the LORD" (v 28). Like Isaiah's vision in the temple, this incredible sight is just a glimpse of God's immense glory.

Have you ever been so awestruck by something you've seen that you haven't been able to find the words to adequately explain it to someone else? This is how Ezekiel feels after his vision.

It would be easy to think that God had totally abandoned his people—after all, they are in exile because they had abandoned him. But in this vision the Lord enters exile, riding on the wings of cherubim, showing Ezekiel that he is not only in heaven but also with his people. Despite their sin against him, he has not left them for ever. One day, he will gather his people back from exile, and give them "an undivided heart and ... a new spirit" so that they will obey him and live as his people again (Ezekiel 11:17-20).

I don't know what dark clouds or bleak days you may be facing right now, but I know there is hope of a brighter day to come. Whether you are experiencing loneliness, illness, anxiety, fear or just the weariness of daily life in a fallen world, the Lord has not abandoned you. He is with you—radiant in glory, mighty to deliver.

Brilliant light surrounds him, like the appearance of a rainbow in the clouds on a rainy day—a radiant symbol of promise and kindness. He will open the heavens and come to us again. There is hope of a brighter day.

Cultivate

Like Isaiah, Ezekiel fell on his face stunned when he saw a vision of God's glory. We are often casual in our approach to him. Is it possible that you have lost sight of the grandeur of the glory of God?

When you next see a rainbow, as well as remembering God's faithfulness to keep his promises, remember Ezekiel's vision and stop to praise him for his radiant glory. What else might serve as a physical reminder of his transcendence?

Pray

Today, if you are able, kneel to pray. Or perhaps try bowing your face to the ground like Ezekiel and Isaiah did. Ask the Lord to give you a greater sense of wonder at his other-worldly glory. Pray that you will grow in reverence as you experience more of him.

4

Radiant Beams

"As he was praying, the appearance of his face changed, and his clothes became as bright as a flash of lightning."

LUKE 9:29

Read Luke 9:18-36

It is possible to know something without really *knowing* it.

The friends had talked together, travelled together, eaten together, weathered turbulent storms together and finally come to the realisation that the man they followed was God's promised Messiah—the one who they hoped would overthrow Israel's enemies, gather God's people, and establish his kingdom on earth. But while they knew this intellectually, they hadn't fully grasped the reality.

Eight days after Peter's confession that Jesus is the Messiah, Jesus takes him, along with James and John, up a mountainside to pray. While they are on the mountaintop, Jesus is suddenly transformed. His face begins to shine like the sun (Matthew 17:2) and his clothes become dazzling white. For a few moments, the radiance and glory of his divine nature breaks through his human form, and his closest friends get to witness it.

Centuries earlier, during the times when God's glory descended on the tent of meeting in the wilderness, Moses would enter the tent to speak with the Lord—and when Moses came out, his face would be radiant (Exodus 34:30, 35). It reflected the brightness of God's glory, just as the moon reflects the sun's beaming light. But on this mountain, Jesus is not simply reflecting God's glory—he *is* the glory! Glory does not descend on him from above; it beams directly out of him. His face, body and clothes radiate light. He is the source of glory—the glorious God himself.

As if this sight isn't enough, Moses and Elijah suddenly appear alongside him "in glorious splendour" (v 30). Don't rush past this moment. Moses has been dead for over 1,400 years, Elijah for over 900, but here they stand on a mountaintop in gloriously restored bodies, talking with Jesus. Both men had previously spoken with God on mountains and seen glimpses of his glory, but here they *share* his glory. In this holy moment, Peter, James and John glimpse a foretaste of what Jesus will do in the future—when he will transform the bodies of all who have believed in him to become like his glorious body (Philippians 3:21). This includes you if you are trusting in Jesus. One day, your body will be renewed and restored so that it resembles something of our risen Lord's glory. What an incredible thought!

How might you have reacted to this revelation of Jesus' splendour? I imagine myself stunned into silence, but Peter is more practical. As Moses and Elijah are leaving, he offers to put up shelters for them and for Jesus. It may have seemed like a noble idea to Peter, but he fails to grasp two important points.

Firstly, Jesus has been talking with Moses and Elijah about "his departure, which he was about to bring to fulfilment at Jerusalem" (Luke 9:31). This is Jesus' death and resurrection—planned from eternity—through which he would secure salvation for his people. Jesus and his disciples must leave the mountaintop if this plan is to be fulfilled. They can't stay there, basking in glory, for ever.

But secondly, Jesus is not simply one more in a long line of prophets speaking God's word to his people. He *is* the Word. The three men can't be grouped together like the presidents on Mount Rushmore because there is no comparison between them. Moses and Elijah had significant roles in Israel's history, but Jesus is the one to whom *all* history points. He is superior in every way. Despite his confession that Jesus is God's Messiah (v 20), Peter doesn't yet *know* this in the depths of his soul. I wonder if you do? Have you really grasped the truth that Jesus is God himself—from eternity to eternity, without beginning or end; supremely glorious, just and true, Lord of lords and King of kings? Why not take a moment now and ask the Holy Spirit to help you understand just how glorious Jesus is.

While Peter is speaking, a cloud envelops the friends and they hear the voice of God the Father:

> *This is my Son, whom I have chosen; listen to him. (v 35)*

There is now no doubt that Jesus is the beloved Son of God, his chosen King (Psalm 2:6-7). And the only right response to this glorious revelation is to listen to what he says. His is the only voice that should captivate us, the only voice we should unequivocally obey. Jesus still speaks to us today through his word and by his Spirit. When we spend time reading the Bible, we are listening to him speak to us through it. We will know him more fully and love him more deeply as we spend time with Jesus and see more of his glory.

Cultivate

When do you find it hard to recognise Jesus as Lord over everything in your life? What other voices sometimes seem louder or more captivating to you than his? Take time to pray about each one, asking the Holy Spirit to help you find Jesus more precious and more worthy of attention than anything or anyone else.

Pray

Lord Jesus, I know you are the true and only Son of God. You are the only one worthy of my wholehearted devotion and unwavering obedience. Please help me see you as you truly are—glorious and majestic—and please help me to love and listen to you. I want to grow in awe of you. Amen.

5

Come Closer

"But you have come to Mount Zion, to the city of the living God, the heavenly Jerusalem … to Jesus the mediator of a new covenant, and to the sprinkled blood that speaks a better word than the blood of Abel."

HEBREWS 12:22-24

Imagine attending a formal dinner at a mansion house. Picture the crisp linen and polished silver; the overwhelming selection of cutlery and glasses that you don't know when to use; fabulously dressed guests; and an austere host who appears to sneer at anyone who doesn't look quite right.

Now contrast that with a casual party at a friend's home. Everyone is relaxed, a pizza slice in one hand and a can of soda in the other. Music is playing; people are chatting and laughing; your friend is beaming, unfazed by noise or mess. You know you are welcome—and feel at home.

As we've been thinking about God's glory, I hope you have been awestruck at the sheer "otherness" of God—his transcendent splendour, the vastness of his being, the unrivalled beauty of his character. But I wonder if the vivid depictions of his greatness and majesty have left you feeling uncertain about your own standing before him. Perhaps you think, *If God is so glorious that even seraphim can't look at him, how can I possibly draw near?*

My hope is that by meditating on the nature of God we will be led to greater awe, not deeper anxiety. Our final passage in this section shows how this is possible. God is more glorious than we can imagine, but he is more approachable than we may think.

Read Hebrews 12:18-24

Do you see the contrast between the way Israel approached God at Mount Sinai and how we now approach him at Mount Zion—the heavenly city where God dwells? You may not have thought about approaching God at Mount Zion before, but this is what we do whenever we pray or sing to him.

When the law was given at Sinai, it was accompanied by such an awesome display of God's glory that the people were terrified (Exodus 19:16-19). They saw a thick cloud shot through with lightning, smoke billowing as if from a fiery furnace. They heard roars of thunder, trumpet blasts, and the voice of God himself. The mountain trembled as he descended—and the people trembled with fear. The sights, sounds and smells of Sinai were terrifying. It was a place of darkness, gloom and storm (Hebrews 12:18).

Mount Zion could not be more different. Although Zion itself was a physical place (the hill Jerusalem was built on), its purpose was always to point to the heavenly city of God—his perfect, permanent dwelling place. Now, Mount Zion is not "a mountain that can be touched" (v 18), but a spiritual mountain that we approach by grace, through faith.

It is not a place of gloom and terror, but a joyful gathering of thousands of angels—and the spirits of believers who have gone ahead of us, now made perfect for ever. Our names are written on the heavenly register with theirs—a reminder that we too will be there one day.

Moses, the mediator of the old covenant, trembled with fear as he approached God at Sinai. But through Jesus, the mediator of the new covenant, we can draw near with joyful confidence. He took our judgment on himself and shed his blood for our forgiveness. The blood of Abel cries out for justice (Genesis 4:10), but Jesus' blood cries for mercy—forgiveness and peace with God for those who trust in him.

While there may be something appealing about the idea of approaching a physical place where we can meet with God, our reality is far greater. We can come close to him in prayer, at any time, confident that he will never turn us away. There is no fear. No dread. No "Please Stand Back!" sign warning us to keep our distance. Rather, we receive a warm welcome from a heavenly Father who loves us.

What is it that keeps you from approaching God with confidence and joy? Perhaps it's an awareness of your sin and unworthiness? At Mount Zion, we are reminded that we have been made perfect through Jesus' sacrifice. Maybe it's doubt that he wants you to draw near? At Mount Zion, we remember he sent his Son to shed his blood and open the way for us to come to him. Maybe it's fear that he is too terrifying to approach? At Mount Zion, we recall the festive crowd of angels and the believers who have gone before us, gathered in joyful celebration without worry or fear.

We may not always be conscious of our hesitation in approaching God, so it's worth pausing to think about it. It is possible to believe these truths in our heads, but deep down to lack the assurance that we really are accepted. But you and I have nothing to fear. Our God is glorious. And he is our Father.

Cultivate

What has most struck you as we have considered God's glory over the last few days? What will help you remember both his "otherness" and our freedom to approach him without fear? Is there a verse you could display somewhere to remind you of his glory?

Pray

Glorious God, you are infinitely superior to me in every way. You are magnificent, splendid, beyond comparison with anything or anyone else in this world. Thank you for revealing yourself to me through your word. And thank you that I do not need to be afraid, but can draw near knowing that you welcome me because of Jesus. Please show me more of your glory as I draw near to you. And, like Moses, help me reflect something of your glory to those around me—that they may worship you too. Amen.

His Power

SHELTERING UNDER GOD'S PROTECTION

6

Our Refuge

"Come and see what the LORD has done, the desolations he has brought on the earth. He makes wars cease to the ends of the earth. He breaks the bow and shatters the spear; he burns the shields with fire."

PSALM 46:8-9

Read through Psalm 46 slowly

What do you feel when you read about the earth and the mountains in verses 2 and 3? For me, there's a sense of horror as I try to visualise this kind of upheaval. These things that we consider immovable and indestructible are upended and destroyed by a roaring, raging sea. We can feel the terror of creation turning on itself; the earth shaking on its foundations, unable to withstand the anger of the waters.

And yet the psalmist says that God's people have no reason to fear—because God is stronger. Think about that for a moment. How powerful must God be if cataclysmic, end-of-world type destructive forces are no match for him? The mountains may crumble, but he remains unmoved. The earth may quake on its foundations, but he remains unshakeable. He is an invincible, unconquerable force.

And he uses his power to protect his people. You may be tempted to shy away from such a powerful being, but the psalmist reminds us that God's omnipotence is good news for those who trust in him. He is not a terror we must run from but a refuge we can run to. He is an always-present, all-powerful help we can turn to in the midst of any trouble (v 1). God's power would be terrifying if it were not matched by his goodness. But because he is good, we can run to him for safety.

In verses 4-7, the psalmist contrasts this life-threatening ocean with the life-giving river that runs through the city of God—the place where he dwells with his people. While the surrounding nations are in uproar, while kingdoms rise and fall, God's people are secure because he is in their midst. A mighty fortress, protecting and providing for them. Ever-present. Ready to help at break of day when the battle begins again.

One of my favourite places to visit is a little Cotswolds village called Bourton-on-the-Water. A perfectly tranquil river runs through the village, crossed by stone arch bridges and shaded by ancient, overhanging tress. The water is clean and clear, shallow enough in places for children (and adults!) to joyfully paddle alongside ducks and other birds. It is beautiful, calm and wonderfully peaceful. A place of rest and delight.

The image of a river of life isn't unique to Psalm 46. Throughout the Bible, from Eden to the New Jerusalem, rivers of living water symbolise the presence of God with his people—providing for them, sustaining them, bringing life and peace. (See Genesis 2; Ezekiel 47; John 4 and 7; Revelation 7 and 21.) It's a comforting image—and a reminder that this indomitable, all-powerful God is compassionate and kind to his people. They can trust him to provide for all they need.

God uses his power to protect his people, but he will also use it to punish those who oppose him. Verses 8-10 are a call to "come and see" what the Lord will do—how he will finally respond to evil. Wars will end. Weapons will be shattered. The wicked will be punished.

But although the final outcome is peace, it is brought about by judgment. "He makes wars cease" not through negotiations but by destroying all that is evil. He will lift his voice against the nations that have raged against him—and they will melt away (v 6) like the mountains of verse 2. He will bring devastation on the earth as he puts an end to injustice, corruption and conflict. He is stronger than the strongest superpower; greater than the greatest political or military leader.

In light of this, the invitation to "be still, and know that I am God" (v 10) is not so much a gentle word of comfort to the restless but a strong rebuke to the warring world. *He* is God. *He* is the omnipotent ruler of the universe. *He* is the one who will be exalted over all.

It's a call for those who war against him to lay down their weapons and submit to him—before it is too late. He, the omnipotent one, will be exalted in the earth. As we witness conflict in our communities and war on our news feeds, we can be sure that he reigns, that he is in control, and that he *will* one day bring an end to all violence and harm. *This* is the God who is with us.

> *The LORD Almighty is with us; the God of Jacob is our fortress. (v 7)*

Cultivate

Read through Psalm 46 again. What images particularly strike you? How do they enlarge your view of God? How does it reassure you to know that this powerful God is for you and not against you?

Listen to "Fortress" by Matt Searles, based on Psalm 46.

Pray

Spend some time praising God for his power. Thank him that he is an immovable, unshakeable refuge in times of trouble.

7

Light and Salvation

"The Lord is my light and my salvation—
whom shall I fear?
The Lord is the stronghold of my life—
of whom shall I be afraid?"

PSALM 27:1

Read Psalm 27

A few years ago, my friend's home was burgled while she and her children were asleep. The intruders didn't enter the bedrooms, but that experience has left her with a deep fear of being alone at night.

I wonder what it is that causes you to fear? Perhaps you're fearful of physical harm that people may do to you or maybe you fear their words, slander or rejection. Often what scares us is related to our past—like my friend experiences. Fear of what people may say or do to us can be paralysing. It can leave us afraid to sleep or afraid to speak. Scared to be alone or anxious in a crowd. What can we look to for security when we feel like this?

Israel's King David also had reasons to feel afraid as he struggled against enemies who wanted to undermine his reign and end his life. But in the face of wicked men, it was the Lord's presence and protection that comforted him. In Psalm 27, David expresses his confidence in God—even as he is confronted by lies and violence (v 12):

> *The LORD is my light and my salvation ...*
> *The LORD is the stronghold of my life. (v 1)*

Throughout the Bible, light symbolises truth, purity, life and joy. Everything good is summed up in this word *light*. David uses it to describe the Lord—*he* is his light, bringing David life and joy and vitality. And he is *our* light too. Evil and fear thrive in darkness, but the Lord banishes the darkness before us and sends his light and truth to lead us safely to his presence (Psalm 43:3).

It may seem as though evil has the upper hand in your life and in our world, but the Lord has won victory over it through the death and resurrection of Jesus. His promise is that all evil will eventually be destroyed and there will be a new heavens and a new earth where righteousness dwells (2 Peter 3:13). Evil won't have the last word.

Psalm 27:1 also tells us that God is a stronghold. The purpose of a stronghold is to protect those who need shelter—it's a place of safety and security. When David calls God the stronghold of his life, he's saying, *The Lord is my place of absolute safety. An impenetrable refuge. Nothing can defeat me when I'm in him.*

> *Though an army besiege me,*
> *my heart will not fear;*
> *though war break out against me,*
> *even then I will be confident. (v 3)*

David's confidence isn't in his ability to defend himself or talk his way out of trouble. He is only confident because the Lord is his refuge. Though he faces wicked individuals (v 2, 12) and mighty armies (v 3), neither frighten him because he knows the Lord is stronger.

And this is true for you too. When you face the words or actions of those who want to cause you pain, you do not need to be afraid because he is the stronghold of *your* life. He is *your* place of safety. *Your* impenetrable refuge. This doesn't mean that no bad thing will ever happen to you—just like we see with David, sometimes the Lord allows us to experience hard things in order to accomplish his purposes for good in our lives. But even in those times, we are safe in his care and no one can disrupt his plans for us. We are eternally secure in him. Is this something you need to remember today? Though people stand against you, the Lord surrounds you. Though your enemies want you to suffer, your God wants you to shelter in him.

David's only request in this psalm is that he will experience the Lord's presence more fully.

One thing I ask from the Lord,
this only do I seek:
that I may dwell in the house of the Lord
all the days of my life,
to gaze on the beauty of the Lord
and to seek him in his temple. (v 4)

He knows God's presence is the place of safety and shelter (v 5). He knows it is the place of victory and joy (v 6). And it's David's knowledge of the Lord's light and strength that fuels his sole desire for his life—a yearning for intimacy with him. If you want to experience the Lord's presence more fully and know the same sense of security David did, make these words your prayer too.

Cultivate

If you're experiencing fear of other people, try to memorise Psalm 27:1. Say it out loud a few times each day—you could write it out on notes and place it around your home to help you. As you recite these words, ask the Spirit to help you believe them fully.

Pray

Lord, you are my light and my salvation—I know I don't need to fear other people. You are my stronghold—help me not to be afraid. When I feel threatened or vulnerable or when people are unkind, please remind me that I can shelter in you, and you will protect me. Help me to be satisfied in your presence and learn to gaze on your goodness. Amen.

8

Stronger Still

"But God made the earth by his power; he founded the world by his wisdom and stretched out the heavens by his understanding. When he thunders, the waters in the heavens roar ... He sends lightning with the rain and brings out the wind from his storehouses."

JEREMIAH 10:12-13

Read Jeremiah 10:6-13

The people of Israel had turned away from the Lord. They had forgotten how he had rescued them from Egypt; how he had lived among them, protecting them from their enemies and providing for their needs. Instead, they had begun to trust in wooden idols dressed in gold and silver, which they carried in their arms. Why did they look to objects they could hold in their pockets and purses for security and peace, rather than relying on the God who had proved his power time and again? It seems laughable, but we do the same thing—not least, with our phones! We may not own wooden idols, but we often look to lifeless created things to meet our needs rather than our powerful Creator.

Jeremiah was a prophet who spoke the word of the Lord to the people of Judah shortly before they were exiled to Babylon. Through Jeremiah, the Lord reminds his wayward people that he alone is great and mighty, the one to whom all other rulers must bow (v 6-7). By his own power, he made the earth—he needed no help. He displays his might in roars of thunder and bolts of lightning that crash through the sky (v 13), calling his creatures to acknowledge him as the true and living God, the eternal King (v 10). He holds the wind in storehouses, ready to be released at his command—and to return at his call.

I don't know about you, but when the wind is blowing, I'm always struck by its power to disturb my peace and disrupt my plans. I'm a light sleeper so I wake at the faintest sound and, once awake, it takes a while to fall back to sleep—especially if it's noisy outside. This last week I've struggled to sleep for more than a few hours each night as high winds have swept through the garden, shaking trees, toppling pots and howling around the windows.

The wind humbles me. It is strong, and I am weak. It blows with unrelenting enthusiasm, while I become quickly wearied. The howling winds and thunderstorms testify to God's power and highlight our own helplessness in contrast. Whether it's physical disabilities, mental difficulties, relational disappointments or spiritual discouragements, we all experience weaknesses that leave us weary. I imagine, like me, you are experiencing some of these struggles right now.

How should weak and weary women relate to an all-powerful God? By humbly acknowledging that he alone is God. By praising him for his awesome power displayed in the wind and storms. By believing that, just as he held back the waters of the Red Sea so the Israelites could escape from Egypt, so he will use his might to bless his precious daughters.

The wind is bold, forceful and intimidating, but it is not all-powerful; it is merely a whispered breath of the one who is. The wind does not determine its own movement; its path is directed by the one who controls all things—the Lord whose mighty strength is displayed in creation; who proves his power as he moves clouds and thunderstorms and lightning flashes throughout the sky. We may not understand why he allows the chaos and destruction caused by tornadoes, typhoons and hurricanes, but we do not need to doubt his power over them. Where else would we place our trust? Who is stronger? Who is wiser?

No one is like you, Lord;
you are great,
and your name is mighty in power. (v 6)

Cultivate

The next time you feel the wind on your face, pause and remember the Lord's power. When you hear a rumble of thunder or see a flash of lightning in the sky, imagine him calling you to behold his might. Stop and declare to your soul that he is awesome and worthy of worship. Compare his strength to your own and confess your reliance on him.

Pray

O Lord, you are great and your name is mighty. No one has power, wisdom or understanding like yours. You are the Creator of the heavens and the earth, the sun, moon and stars. You display your might in the roar of thunder and cracks of lightning. You reveal your power in howling winds and torrents of rain. Help me live in awe of your greatness. Teach me to fear your name for there is none like you. When I am tempted to admire lesser gods, remind me of your power and cause me to marvel at your might. Amen.

9

Who Is This?

"Who is this? Even the wind and the waves obey him!"

MARK 4:41

Towards the end of Mark 4, Jesus' disciples learn something about him that leaves them astounded. They have been with Jesus a little while and have seen him heal the sick and drive out demons, but they haven't yet grasped the magnitude of his power and authority.

Read Mark 4:35-41

Jesus has been teaching by a lake. In the evening, he and his disciples leave the crowd and set sail. As they cross the lake, a violent storm arises with waves so high they threaten to swamp and sink the boat. From a human perspective, the disciples have every reason to be afraid. The experienced fishermen among them know the danger they are in if the storm does not subside. But what they don't know is that Jesus is immeasurably more powerful than the storm.

While he sleeps, they panic. They mistake his peace for indifference: "Teacher, don't you care if we drown?" (v 38). They fear a created power over the one who created it. They don't know that he is the one who "brings out the wind from his storehouses" (Jeremiah 10:13).

When I was a high-school teacher, there was a girl in one of my classes who was painfully shy. She worked silently and avoided eye contact. If I asked her a question, she mumbled so quietly that I could barely hear the answer, her face flushed with embarrassment. When she turned up to audition for the school musical one year, I was surprised. How would she be able to perform in front of hundreds of people when she struggled to speak in a class of 30?

I played the intro for her audition piece, preparing myself for a painful try-out. But as soon as she opened her mouth, I realised I had underestimated her. Her voice was flawless. She sang with power, emotion and a hauntingly beautiful tone. Everyone in the room was transfixed, my co-workers and I gazing at her in amazement. We had no idea that this timid young girl had such incredible ability.

When Jesus rebukes the wind and commands the waves, the extraordinary happens: they obey. The wind dies down and all is calm. A different kind of fear descends as the disciples wonder, "Who is this?" (v 41). They begin to see that their teacher has absolute power over all things—and they are amazed. If even the wind and waves obey him, is there anything he cannot do? Anything he cannot control?

This is awe. Earthly fear displaced by reverent fear of the one who holds supreme power. One who will use his power for their good. Jesus shows that he is far more than a wise teacher and miraculous healer—nothing can overwhelm him. Nothing threatens him. Nothing is stronger than him. The most perilous storm is simply an opportunity for him to demonstrate his power and protect his friends.

Jesus' power over the wind and waves proves he is God and worthy of worship.

Are there times when you underestimate Jesus? I know I do. We can know in our heads that he is the all-powerful God, but this knowledge doesn't always make its way to our hearts. We doubt whether Jesus really can help us—and whether he even wants to. We may find ourselves echoing the disciples' question, *Teacher, don't you care?*

Don't you care if I lose my job? Don't you care if I'm sick? Don't you care if my friend betrays me or my family disowns me or my church disappoints me?

It's easy to become overwhelmed by earthly fears—the loss of health, income, relationships, stability or security. What people think or say about you. Making mistakes, being humiliated, being the cause of pain to others. Perhaps your greatest fear is death.

What will free you from these earthly fears and enable you to live in freedom and joy? Only the reverent fear of a Saviour who is strong enough to rescue and willing to save. A Saviour who has proved he is more powerful than even death—who uses his power to protect and provide for those precious to him.

Jesus was willing to face the greatest storm of all—the righteous wrath of God against sin—so we never have to. He relinquished his power for our sake, becoming unimaginably weak, but when the time was right, he used his mighty power to overthrow the reign of death and darkness. His power has been used only for our good and our salvation. So we can trust him to continue to work in mysterious ways for our good now.

When we turn our gaze away from the storms that threaten to overwhelm us and towards the one who is in the boat with us and has power to protect us, worry is replaced with worship. Anxiety gives way to awe.

Cultivate

What earthly situations feel big and overwhelming to you today? Consider Jesus' power over the natural and supernatural world. List some of the ways he demonstrated this power when he was on earth. Compare his power with the things you dread. Which is greater?

Listen to the song "One Word", by Melanie Penn.

Pray

Write a short prayer confessing your fears to the Lord and asking him to replace it with a reverent fear of him.

10

Held Secure

"To him who is able to keep you from stumbling and to present you before his glorious presence without fault and with great joy."

JUDE 24

Read Jude 17-25

As I've reflected on God's power over the last few days, I've begun to feel rather small. As we've compared his strength with mighty mountains and storming seas, I've felt my own feebleness and fragility. As we've marvelled at his control over every part of this world, I've been struck by my inability to control the circumstances of my own life. Maybe you feel the same.

When we see God more clearly, we begin to view ourselves with greater clarity than before—and it is humbling. C.S. Lewis said:

> *In God you come up against something which is in every respect immeasurably superior to yourself.*[1]

Do you feel that way as you reflect on the immensity of his power?

But there is also a comfort in understanding his power, because we have seen that God uses his power for good. He is a God who promises to work for our benefit—and he has power to keep his word. This is our reassurance as we face situations that are outside of our control. Knowing that he will be my strength when I am weak, my place of safety and security in the face of every danger, an immovable, unshakeable rock when people are unreliable and circumstances are overwhelming, enables me to walk through life with confidence and joy.

There are times, though, when my faith feels feeble. Do you ever find yourself looking at other women in your church family and feeling inadequate or ashamed because they appear unwavering in their faith while you often wrestle with doubts and unanswered questions? Or do you listen to other women sharing encouragements from God's word or stories about his faithfulness in hard times, and wonder why you can't muster up a more joyful, hopeful perspective in suffering? Do you sometimes wonder whether you will persevere and make it to the end? These kinds of doubts and comparisons can affect us all.

Knowledge of God's power gives us hope, not only when we are physically weak but also when we feel spiritually weak. The last two verses of Jude's letter hold out hope to those who fear their faith may fail: God is able to keep us from stumbling and enable us to stand in his presence on the final day—without fear and without fault. Not because our faith is unwavering but because he is. Not because we have the strength to stand firm in the face of pressure or pain, but because his power can hold us steady.

We are not strong enough to secure our own salvation—or to lose it! It is our mighty God who will keep us in his love and enable us to stand confident and unashamed in the presence of his glory. One day, he will present us before his throne with great joy. On that day, we will rejoice that his power has kept us safe and brought us home. We will celebrate his victory over sin and death; his might in raising Jesus from the dead. We will delight in his power to banish pain, suffering, fears and tears—for ever.

You may feel weak and your faith may be unsteady, but you can have absolute confidence that you will make it to the end. The power that raised Christ from the dead lives in you (Ephesians 1:19-20) and can strengthen you so that you may have great endurance and patience (Colossians 1:11). His power can bring to fruition your desire to do good and the work produced by your faith, so that Jesus is glorified in you (2 Thessalonians 1:11). You don't need to be strong: his strength is sufficient.

How should we respond to this wonderful truth? Jude gives us the words:

> *To the only God our Saviour be glory, majesty, power and authority, through Jesus Christ our Lord, before all ages, now and for evermore! Amen. (Jude 25)*

Cultivate

In what ways do you feel spiritually weak? How does a deeper understanding of God's power strengthen your faith and trust in him? Take some time to reflect on his power to keep you until the end.

Pray

Mighty and all-powerful God, I praise you that you will keep me to the end and, by your power, present me before your glorious presence without fault and with great joy. All glory and praise be to you, through Jesus Christ my Lord. Amen.

His Creation

WONDERING AT GOD'S DESIGN

11

The Master Artist

"By the word of the Lord *the heavens were made,*
their starry host by the breath of his mouth."

PSALM 33:6

The first time I heard Rachmaninov's Piano Concerto No. 2, I was mesmerised. As strong opening chords gave way to a flowing melody, which hurtled with lightning speed towards the dramatic ending, I kept thinking, "Wow! How did he create that? What incredible talent!"

Great art naturally creates great awe—whether music, poetry or a striking painting. But God's artwork is even more breathtaking.

My daughter has a print of Van Gogh's *Starry Night* on her bedroom wall. It's a striking picture and there's no doubt (in my mind, at least) that Van Gogh was a creative genius. But he didn't invent the starry night; his inspiration came from real stars in the sky that God himself created—*by the breath of his mouth.*

Read Psalm 33:6-9

Unlike Van Gogh, or any other creator, God did not receive inspiration from another source. Rather, *he* is the source of his own creativity. He is the only artist to create *ex nihilo,* that is, from nothing. He needed no paint or clay; he used no template or pre-determined structure. With his voice he brought into being the universe with its billions of galaxies, solar systems, stars and planets—each its own unique marvel:

For he spoke, and it came to be;
he commanded, and it stood firm. (v 9)

If this feels too much to get your head around, that's because it is! This kind of creation is inconceivable to us as human beings. Even the most gifted artist, musician or inventor creates from knowledge and materials that have been given to them. No one has ever made even a tiny object appear simply by speaking. But God made everything we can see—and everything we can't—by his word.

God made stars by the breath of his mouth—imagine him blowing out giant exploding balls of gas the way a child blows soap bubbles from their little wand! He scoops the rolling seas into jars and gathers them in storehouses—like a cook filling a pantry with endless jars of rice and flour and olive oil.

We can't begin to comprehend the magnitude of our own small galaxy that is 100,000 light-years wide and contains over 100 billion stars, let alone the vastness of the whole universe. But what is even more amazing is that God individually sees, knows and cares about you and me:

From heaven the L*ORD looks down*
and sees all mankind;
from his dwelling-place he watches
all who live on earth—
he who forms the hearts of all,
who considers everything they do. (v 13-15)

This same magnificent Creator knows you intimately. You may feel insignificant—perhaps, at times, unseen by people around you. But God has formed your heart—like a miniature work of art—and he keeps you in his sight. So whatever you do today and whatever you face, this psalm tells you that you are seen and valued by the Lord of all.

The works of his hand are more awesome than any Van Gogh painting or Beethoven symphony. When we gaze on the beauty of creation, we can wonder at the God who speaks artistry into being, yet whose eyes are on those who fear him (v 18), so we can put our hope "in his unfailing love" (v 18, 22).

Cultivate

The next time you are moved by a work of art, a piece of music or some beautiful writing, thank God for the creative gifts he has given those whose work you admire. Then remind yourself that he is the true source of beauty and the only artist who creates from nothing. Imagine him speaking stars and planets, trees and rivers into being. Praise him for his unlimited imagination and his generosity in creating such a vast and surprising universe.

Pray

Lord God, you are the true master artist. There is no limit to your imagination or creative power. You speak beauty, goodness and order into being; you uphold the universe by the power of your word. How wonderful are your works! How limitless your power! How incomprehensible your divine nature! When I consider the universe you imagined and spoke into being, I am amazed. No one but you could do it—you are truly awesome. When I remember that you know and care about me, I am overwhelmed with gratitude. How precious it is to be known and loved by you. Amen.

12

Eternal Language

"How many are your works, Lord!
In wisdom you made them all;
the earth is full of your creatures."

PSALM 104:24

A few months ago, I was running through the woods near my home with a friend. Surrounded by majestic trees, sweet-smelling bushes, and a spectacular carpet of bluebells, I was awestruck by the divine nature and power of God.

Except, I wasn't. Rather, I was complaining about the persistently dull, white-grey sky and the chill in the air. Earlier that day, another friend had posted photos on Instagram of a vividly blue Colorado sky, taken from her front porch. My running partner and I agreed we would find it much easier to live with a sense of wonder if our homes were located somewhere with reliably blue skies and dramatic mountain ranges.

Perhaps you do live somewhere like that. Or maybe, like me, the view from your window is less breathtaking. Either way, we are all prone to lose our sense of wonder at the world around us. If that's how you are feeling, let Psalm 104 reawaken your delight—both in creation itself, and the God behind it all.

Read Psalm 104

The poet Samuel Taylor Coleridge described creation as God's "eternal language". Through it he reveals his invisible qualities—his eternal power and divine nature—so that we may know him (Romans 1:20). Do you ever stop to "listen" to what he might be saying through the world he created?

The psalmist not only marvels at God's power in creation; he is also struck by his care for every part of it. He causes springs to flow into valleys, providing water for the beasts of the fields and the birds of the air (Psalm 104:10-12). They may appear to look after themselves, but they are completely dependent on their Creator to supply their every need.

He makes grass grow so that cattle may feed, and plants so that people may grow food for themselves (v 14). He provides wine, oil and bread—to sustain and satisfy us. Even the mighty cedar trees of Lebanon are planted and cared for by him—and within their branches the birds find a home. God has not simply set things in motion and left his created world to run its course. If he had, that would still be amazing, but even more amazingly, he continues to sustain and provide for all he has made. He gives detailed care and attention to every creature—from the greatest to the least.

All creatures look to you
to give them their food at the proper time …
when you open your hand,
they are satisfied with good things. (v 27-28)

If you've ever owned pets, you'll know how much work can be involved in caring for them. My husband and I are not pet people but, when my son was young, he was desperate for an animal to care for, so we allowed him to get a couple of guinea pigs. A friend who is a vet promised me they would be easy to look after and wouldn't cost much to keep. He was wrong! They needed a steady supply of food and water, a clean hutch and plenty of hay for warmth. They needed regular attention and play—when my son ignored them, they would fight each other. Eventually, when one almost killed the other, they needed visits to the vet, medication, and separating into two hutches (more expense!). This "low-maintenance" pair of tiny creatures were a handful and I was not too sad when their time with us came to an end. Of course, we are much more of a handful than guinea pigs, with our sinful behaviour, chaos and wars. But we cannot be too much for God—he has dealt with all our mess and never tires of caring for us.

In our modern world, we can forget how dependent we are on the Lord. Most of us in the West don't collect water from a stream or grow our own food—so we forget how much we rely on him to water the earth and to make the grass and plants grow. Perhaps we need to take more time to look at creation and consider the ways he shows tender care for it all.

As I write, the sky is dull and grey again. But I'm reminded that the psalmist didn't go to far-off places to awaken wonder; he simply looked around him and marvelled at what his eyes could see—and the God who made it all.

Cultivate

Once a week, try to get outside and recite Psalm 104:24. As you do, look closely at some of the Lord's works around you: songbirds, squirrels, snails—ordinary creatures depending on an extraordinary Creator. Consider his wisdom in making them just the way they are, and his care in providing for all he has made.

Pray

Father, I confess I am often slow to praise you for the wisdom and power I see in creation. You have made a world full of wonders—and I complain about the weather. You sustain and care for all you have made—and I grumble that I have dishes to wash and laundry to fold. Open my eyes to the wonders in front of me each day; cause me to marvel at your greatness and goodness. Fuel my desire to worship you as I consider your works. Amen.

13

I Don't Know, but He Does!

"Where were you when I laid the earth's foundation?"

"Who laid its cornerstone—while the morning stars sang together and all the angels shouted for joy?"

JOB 38:4, 6-7

How does growing in awe of God help us during times of trial and suffering?

As I write, a dear friend is dying of cancer. Doctors have tried various treatments, but nothing is working. The news keeps getting worse and her suffering is unrelenting. You probably know someone in a similar situation—or perhaps you are in the midst of an intense trial yourself. If that is the case, I am so sorry. In times of affliction it is hard to know where to turn for genuine comfort. Well-worn clichés offer little consolation. We need a stronger answer to our questions and complaints.

The Old Testament story of Job points us in the right direction. Job experiences excruciating pain and devastating loss. In one day, he loses his wealth, his livelihood and all his children. Then he is afflicted with painful sores all over his body. He is repulsive to his wife, rejected by his family, and ridiculed by children. Most of his friends stay away, and those who sit with him blame him for his suffering. After contesting their claims that he is reaping the rewards of an unrighteous life, Job appeals to the Lord to affirm his innocence or prove his guilt.

The Lord does neither. Instead, he asks questions of his own—not to increase Job's agitation, but to lead him to deeper awe. Through a series of rapid-fire, rhetorical questions, he graciously leads Job to see his wisdom revealed through creation.

Read Job 38:4-11, 22-41; 39:1-12

The Lord questions Job about his knowledge of the foundations of the earth; the constellations of the stars; the places where snow and hail are stored; the sources of rain and ice. He invites him to discuss the hunting strategies of lions and the birthing habits of goats; the foolishness of wild donkeys and the strength of horses.

His intent is not to humiliate Job by forcing him to answer "No" or "I don't know" to every question. Rather, it is to lead him to acknowledge, *I wasn't there, but you were! I don't know, but you know! I can't control anything, but you rule it all!*

There is deep comfort and great freedom in acknowledging the sovereign rule of the Creator. It is humbling to confess that we do not have sufficient knowledge or power to rule our own lives, and this kind of humility leads to joyful submission to the one who does. Job could not answer the Lord's questions—and neither can you or I. But we don't need to! The point is that as Creator, God has complete knowledge of every part of this world—and it is an intimate knowledge. He is not distant or disinterested but close and compassionate. Even the things that make no sense to you or I are known, and lovingly tended to, by him.

How does growing in awe of God as the Creator help us in times of trial and suffering? It teaches us humility to acknowledge we do not know or understand the purpose behind pain—but the Lord does. It reminds us we are a small part of a big story—but are loved and valued, nonetheless. It helps us trust the Lord to complete his work in our lives—and to lead us through pain into glory.

Cultivate

Listen to "Out of the Whirlwind" by Co-Mission.

What words from the song will help you to find wonder in knowing that God's wisdom is so much greater than yours—especially when life is hard or confusing?

Pray

Write a prayer of lament:

- Tell the Lord what circumstances are confusing you or causing you pain.
- Acknowledge your inability to understand what he is doing, and confess any doubts you may have about his goodness in these situations.
- Recall his wisdom in creation—list some of the things he has knowledge of that you don't.
- Ask him to help you believe that he is wise and knows exactly what he is doing—even though you don't.
- Ask for faith to trust him through the storms and trials that come your way.
- Praise him that he is sovereign over them all.

14

Made Visible

"All things have been created through him and for him."

COLOSSIANS 1:16

In the 2005 film adaptation of Jane Austen's *Pride and Prejudice,* there is a sculpture gallery in the Darcy family home filled with marble statues and busts—including one of Mr Darcy himself. As Lizzie Bennet studies Darcy's marble features, viewers get the sense that she is forced to acknowledge not only that he is "a handsome man" (as the housekeeper points out) but also the warmth and kindness suggested in the sculptor's portrayal of him—characteristics Lizzie has previously failed to notice.

A good sculptor aims to do more than simply create a 3-D representation of a person's physical features; they try to capture their subject's mood or temperament. But no artist, however talented, can capture all of a subject's virtues, emotions or personality traits.

This is even more true when it comes to God. It is impossible to represent him in a way that captures even a fraction of his transcendence. But in his grace he made himself visible so we might know him more fully.

Read Colossians 1:15-18

Jesus is the image of the invisible God—not an artist's interpretation but the actual revelation of God himself. "Firstborn over all creation" doesn't mean that Christ was simply the first to be created—that makes no sense if he is the one who did the creating! It means that Christ is first in rank. All honour belongs to him. He has supremacy over everything and everyone—because, though he has been clothed in human flesh, he is the one who made it all.

For everything was created by him,
in heaven and on earth,
the visible and the invisible,
whether thrones or dominions
or rulers or authorities—
all things have been created through him and for him.
(v 16, CSB)

Every creature on earth—from giant African bush elephants to tiny Etruscan shrews—was created by Christ. So also were the things in the heavenly realms that we can't see: "thrones or dominions or rulers or authorities". Elsewhere in Scripture and in Jewish literature, these descriptions refer to classes of angelic powers—rulers and authorities being the highest (Ephesians 3:10; 6:12; Colossians 2:15). Even the highest order of angels are subject to Christ.

Christ is also the *reason* for creation—everything has been created for him. Not because he needs any of it—as God, he has no needs at all. But so that every part of creation—on earth and in the spiritual realm—may honour and glorify him as Lord of all. We don't always see this happening now, but one day everyone will bow before him and acknowledge that he is Lord (Philippians 2:11). If Christ were just another human like you or I, this may not feel like a good thing—it would seem self-serving at best and dangerous at worst for someone to create people purely to bring themselves glory. But because he is God and, as such, totally pure and infinitely loving, we don't need to feel uncomfortable about it. (Later, we will focus on the awesome kindness of God, and we will see that everything he is and does is rooted in that.)

If everything is made by Christ and for him, that includes you and me. We were created to bring glory to him. This means everything we do should honour him in some way. On the one hand, this could seem too great a responsibility to handle. But on the other, it gives great purpose and value to the ordinary work of our daily lives. No task is irrelevant if it is done with the goal of honouring Jesus. Nothing is meaningless if it is done with him in mind.

I was reminded of this recently while cleaning my kitchen window. It's a boring job, and not always noticed by my family. But as I stood at the window, wiping away splash marks and rubbing the glass until it shone, I offered a prayer of thanksgiving—for the cleansing work of Christ in my own life, his humility in coming into our world as a servant, and the opportunity to reflect his beauty and grace in small ways to my family, friends and neighbours.

Lastly, Paul reminds us that Christ is also the one who sustains all things—without his sustaining work, everything would fall apart. Despite how it may sometimes seem, this world is not falling apart; Jesus Christ is holding things together—just as he always has. And he will continue to do so. He is Lord of all.

Cultivate

Consider what it means to be created by Christ for the express purpose of bringing glory to him. Is there a task this week that you could do with renewed purpose and vigour because you want to honour him? Is there a relationship you could approach from a different perspective as you remember that he is Lord of all?

Pray

Lord Jesus, all things exist for your glory, and I want to glorify you with my life. Please help me to honour you in the way you deserve. Teach me to be mindful of you as I go about my daily life. Show me how to bring glory to you through my work, my rest, my relationships and responsibilities. Help me remember that you are the only one worthy of all my praise and adoration. Amen.

15

Sing, Always

"You are worthy, our Lord and God, to receive glory and honour and power, for you created all things, and by your will they were created and have their being."

REVELATION 4:11

I love to sing—and I love listening to others sing too. Last week my grown children came home for a study break and the house was filled with music all day long. I was introduced to songs I didn't know as they sang along with their favourite bands, but what brought me most joy was hearing my children singing songs of praise and worship to God.

Throughout history, God's people have expressed their wonder at creation by singing songs of praise to the Creator—some written by biblical authors (like Psalms 33 and 104); others by Christians across the world and throughout the centuries. Singing to God helps us to orient our thoughts on the right things, and it fuels our awe of him as we recount his greatness and goodness in memorable ways. (Have you noticed how you can remember words you have sung more easily than words you have read?)

Singing is a natural response to our Creator—not only on earth but also in heaven. Towards the end of his life, the apostle John is given a vision of God's heavenly throne room. It is a breathtaking sight, glimpses of which we have already seen in the visions described by Isaiah and Ezekiel.

Read Revelation 4:1-11

Did you notice that God's throne is central to John's vision? Everything else revolves around it—including the worshippers. Nearest are the living creatures, similar to those in Ezekiel's vision, who continually praise God saying, "Holy, holy, holy is the Lord God Almighty, who was, and is, and is to come" (v 8).

Next are the 24 elders, most likely representing all God's people. They are seated on their own thrones, dressed in white and wearing gold crowns. As the living creatures praise God for his holiness, the elders lay their crowns before his throne and worship with their own song:

You are worthy, our Lord and God,
to receive glory and honour and power,
for you created all things,
and by your will they were created
and have their being. (v 11)

Recently, a friend commented that the word "worthy" is rarely used in contemporary speech. We talked about ways it may have been used by previous generations to describe what someone is deserving of, or what it is fitting or appropriate to say or do to them. In this heavenly scene, the elders recognise that God is worthy to receive glory and honour and power because not only did he make everything but he is the originator of creation. No one asked or persuaded him to create; the desire was his alone and he alone is the one who accomplished it. So it is right and appropriate that he receive worship from his creatures.

Perhaps when you read or sing songs like these seen in Revelation, you wonder how God can receive from his creatures attributes he already possesses to an infinite degree. It is not as if he is somehow lacking in glory, honour or power that he should receive more from you or me! What he can receive, though, is our praise, wonder, adoration and enjoyment of him. Acclamation that he alone is glorious, honourable and powerful. We can celebrate his radiant beauty, delight in his incomparable worth, and marvel at his magnificent power.

God doesn't need to receive honour or acclamation from us, but the truth is, we need to give it. He doesn't benefit from our praise, but we benefit from offering it. As we articulate what is true about his nature and character, we grow in our delight and trust of him. As we retell stories of his mercy and kindness, our faith is strengthened, our hope is renewed and our love is rekindled. God is not changed in any way by receiving our praise, but we are changed as we offer it to him with sincere and thankful hearts. And a joyful, memorable way to do that is in song.

I imagine you sing every Sunday at church, but what about during the week? Our days are often filled with worries, disappointments or frustrations—usually to do with things we have no control over. But singing praise to our Creator can refocus our attention on what is good and beautiful, and keep us from cynicism or despair. It can train our hearts to rejoice rather than grumble. It can awaken awe when we have become lethargic.

Cultivate

Create a playlist of songs that focus specifically on God's work in creation. Play it while you are walking, driving, washing-up or doing other chores. Sing along and delight loudly in your Creator. (If it helps, you could imagine yourself singing to him in his heavenly throne room.) Share it with a friend and invite her to praise him with you.

Pray

You are worthy, O Lord our God,
to receive glory and honour and power.
For you created all things,
and they exist because you created what you pleased.
(v 11, NLT)

His Uniqueness

KNOWING NOTHING COMPARES TO GOD

16

He Counts the Stars

"To whom will you compare me?
Or who is my equal?"

ISAIAH 40:25

Where are you, God? Why don't you do something to stop this?

Have you asked either of those questions recently? Perhaps when watching news reports of fighting and war, poverty and injustice. Maybe when the suffering in your own life, or in the lives of those you love, seems overwhelming and unrelenting. I have cried out to the Lord like this as I've watched dear friends suffer unimaginable pain and loss and wondered why he wouldn't intervene to spare them such grief.

If you find yourself despairing over situations that are outside of your control, you are not alone. But there is comfort for our suffering and relief for our despair as we lift our gaze to behold our God.

In chapter 2, we thought about how God is different to you or I—he is totally other. Perhaps it is unsurprising that Isaiah, the prophet who was mesmerised by the train of God's glory filling the temple, is the one who later exhorts people facing exile to lift their eyes and behold their God. In chapter 40, Isaiah paints a stunning picture of the God who is like no other. He is truly incomparable.

Read Isaiah 40:12-26

Isaiah's words are intended to comfort the people of Judah in their distress—and they can settle our hearts too.

He is the God who can hold the world's oceans in the hollow of his hand and measure the skies between his thumb and little finger. He carries the dust of the earth in a basket, and weighs mountains and hills on measuring scales—like a fruit seller weighing apples and pears. From his throne, far above the earth's circle, we appear as small as grasshoppers (v 22) and as powerless as ants. Strong nations are like drops of water in a bucket; earth's islands like specks of dust (v 15). Compared to him, the greatest princes and the most ruthless rulers of our world are like balls of fluff, swept away to nothing in the breeze:

They shrivel when God blows on them.
Like flecks of chaff, they're gone with the wind.
(v 24, The Message)

He formed the stars and calls them out every night. Each one answers to its name—Antares, Arcturus, Atlas, Atria…

Because of his great power and incomparable strength,
not a single one is missing. (v 26, NLT)

This is our God! He is incomparable but not inaccessible. Awesome, yet approachable. Far above us, but not far removed from us. Around 700 years after Isaiah encouraged the people of Judah to behold their God, Jesus came—speaking words of wisdom, performing works of power, revealing the heart of God to us (John 1:18).

As we look at Jesus' life on earth, we can see vividly that our God is not only sovereign, powerful and wise—he is also loving and gracious. And he invites us to know and trust him. So what if, in the face of confusing circumstances or painful problems, we learn to ask a different question? Instead of, "Why, Lord?" maybe we could ask, "Who are you, Lord?" Instead of demanding an explanation for the things we don't understand, perhaps we could seek a greater revelation of his glory.

> *For God, who said, "Let light shine out of darkness," made his light shine in our hearts to give us the light of the knowledge of God's glory displayed in the face of Christ.*
> *(2 Corinthians 4:6)*

Cultivate

Read Isaiah 40:12-26 again slowly. Highlight (either in your Bible or on a printed copy) the characteristics of God that set him apart from anyone or anything else. Try to think of a specific way one (or more) of these truths could change the way you view situations you struggle to make sense of.

Pray

Write a prayer confessing the things you struggle to understand about the ways God is (or doesn't appear to be) working in your own life or in the lives of others. Ask him to give you a deeper understanding of who he is and a greater trust in his wisdom, power, sovereignty and goodness. Thank him that he wants to be known by you and ask him to help you seek him more and more.

17

His Faithful Plan

"I am God, and there is no other;
I am God, and there is none like me."

ISAIAH 46:9

In my teens, I read several books about how to discern God's will for my life. I heard people say that God had a good plan for my life—and I didn't want to miss it! There were so many big decisions ahead—what to study, what universities to apply to, what career to pursue, what church to choose, which friends to live with. It felt like there were endless opportunities to either miss or to mess up God's plans for me.

Read Isaiah 46:3-13

Part of what it means for God to be God is that he (and only he) decides what will take place long before it actually happens—and then brings it about. This includes the big events of our universe and the small events of our lives. It isn't simply that God knows in advance what will happen. He is not a fortune-teller claiming to predict the future by gazing into a cosmic crystal ball or reading celestial tea leaves. Rather, he is in total control of it.

> *My purpose will stand, and I will do all that I please.*
> *(v 10)*

The reason God knows the future is that he planned it! How does that make you feel? I imagine it raises some questions about sin, sickness and suffering. We have to honestly acknowledge that with our finite understanding we will never be able to answer all of those questions fully—and it is beyond the scope of this book to attempt to do so. But alongside these questions is assurance that the world is not "going to hell in a handbasket". Rather, it is in the sovereign control of a good God—whose word can be trusted, whose ways are perfect, and whose nature is love.

In verses 3-7, the Lord contrasts the futility of trusting in false gods to the security of trusting in him. People use their gold and silver to create gods that they can carry on their shoulders and display in their homes. They pay for them with their own hard-earned money—and then devote themselves to worshipping them.

We do this too—we spend money on clothes, activities, gadgets and accessories—and look to them to meet needs that they cannot meet. They may bring some joy, but they have no power to rescue us from trouble or trials. Like Israel's gods of gold and silver, they look good but are unable to answer prayer.

But while we carry these powerless little gods around on our shoulders (or in our bags and pockets!), the Lord carries us in his mighty arms. He will not weaken or grow weary. He has carried us since we were born (v 3), and will continue to carry us for the rest of our days (v 4). He will be faithful to sustain and rescue those who follow him—and nothing will derail his plans for them:

> *What I have said, that I will bring about;*
> *what I have planned, that I will do.* (v 11)

These words promise deliverance for God's people from their exile in Babylon. The Lord will bring this about through a man "from a far-off land" (v 11) called Cyrus (45:1, 13). But the promise is also about a greater deliverance, because the people's greatest problem is not their circumstances but their hearts—they are far from his righteousness (46:12). There is nothing they can do to save themselves from sin, so he promises to bring salvation to them:

> *I am bringing my righteousness near,*
> *it is not far away;*
> *and my salvation will not be delayed.*
> *I will grant salvation to Zion, my splendour to Israel.* (v 13)

And this promise is also for us. Though, like the Israelites, we are unfaithful and cling to powerless things for security and satisfaction, God remains faithful to the promises and salvation plan he had for us since before the creation of the world (Ephesians 1:4-5, 11). Though, like the Israelites, our hearts are far from righteous, we are now in possession of Jesus' perfect righteousness. While we will want to be wise and godly in our decision-making, we don't need to fear that we will mess up our lives; we have seen God's loving promise fulfilled in Jesus and we can be confident that he is able to fulfil his every good purpose.

Cultivate

When your circumstances feel out of your control or you're anxious about making wrong decisions and missing God's plan for your life, pause and picture him carrying you through the various stages of life—as a helpless baby, as a young girl at school, through your teenage years and into womanhood. Picture him carrying you safely through the rocky terrain of sickness, financial instability, broken relationships and mental health challenges. Finally, picture him carrying you through the dark valley of death and out the other side into eternal life.

Pray

Lord, you alone are God. Thank you that your purposes will stand and you will accomplish all you have planned. I praise you for Jesus and for his incredible sacrifice, so I can have confidence that you will do all you have promised. Help me to trust you when I don't understand your ways, and keep me from trusting in anything or anyone else to save and sustain me. Amen.

18

An Undivided Heart

"You are great and do marvellous deeds;
you alone are God."

PSALM 86:10

Recently, I was talking with a friend about growing in awe of God. She said to me, "I can see how it would be a good thing to cultivate greater awe of God, but I'm not sure it's something I should be trying to do now. I find the Christian life hard enough—I'm not ready to move on to the heavy stuff!"

My friend has been a Christian for a long time but has always struggled with assurance and doubt. She feels that until she has a "more steady faith" she will not be able to know God deeply—so there is no point trying. Another friend expressed similar thoughts. She is sure of her salvation but finds daily life wearying and wrestles with discontentment and discouragement. She wonders if she will more naturally grow in awe when her circumstances are less challenging. I've sometimes thought that cultivating awe does seem like a lower priority—surely it's not as important as cultivating love or peace or patience or generosity? Are any of these feelings familiar to you?

However, I've found that it is possible to cultivate awe even in the midst of difficult or disappointing circumstances. In fact, it is not only possible but necessary if we are to see beyond what our emotions tell us. The psalmists regularly interrupt their cries of lament to God and their prayers for his deliverance with exclamations of praise as they remind themselves of who God is and why he is worthy of worship. This is what David does in Psalm 86:

> *Arrogant foes are attacking me, O God;*
> *ruthless people are trying to kill me. (v 14)*

We don't know exactly what circumstances prompt David to write this particular psalm, but he is clearly under attack from ungodly people who want him dead. In verses 1-7 and 14-17, David cries out for the Lord to have mercy and save him from his troubles. But between these petitions is praise.

Read Psalm 86:8-13

Commenting on this psalm, the 16th-century Reformer Martin Luther wrote:

> *Notice how abundantly and masterly [David] praises God and refers to his goodness, loyalty, and power in order to warm up his faith and heat up his prayer. We should do the same.*[2]

If you feel your passion for the Lord has cooled and the fire of your faith feels more sputtering than blazing, pause now and pray that contemplating the uniqueness of God will warm you too.

Among the gods there is none like you, Lord;
no deeds can compare with yours. (v 8)

Throughout history there have been rulers who set themselves up as gods and demanded unwavering devotion and allegiance. But all of these leaders have died! The New Testament refers to Satan and his demons as gods of this world (1 Corinthians 8:5; 10:20; 2 Corinthians 4:4) who may wield power for a limited time. But they cannot create from nothing, give life, forgive sins and secure salvation. There may be people in our lives who appear to have power to manipulate our circumstances and make us feel small. But however powerful or intimidating these individuals may be, only God is God!

One day, all the nations will recognise God's greatness and honour him as Lord (Psalm 86:9). What an encouragement this is when we feel weak in sharing our faith or disheartened by the persecution of the global church. Jesus' great commission to make disciples of all nations will not fail—its success is guaranteed!

To fuel his faith, David affirms God's greatness in the heavenly realms, in nature, among the nations of the world and throughout history. In other words—over every person, in every place, for all time! David's reflections on the uniqueness of his God lead him to pray for an undivided heart. But he doesn't wait for the answer to that prayer before he determines to praise and glorify God:

I will praise you, Lord my God, with all my heart;
I will glorify your name for ever. (v 12)

David commits to delighting in the Lord right then and there—rather than delaying until his circumstances or emotions have changed. And when we do the same, our outlook begins to change too. Instead of waiting until we're more steady or peaceful or godly, we can choose to seek awe in him right where we are and let our vision of God become bigger than the problems we see in front of us. We can trust that, when we ask him, the Lord will answer our prayer for a renewed heart.

Cultivate

When does it feel hardest to focus your attention on what sets the Lord apart from lesser "gods"? Come up with a prompt (perhaps a word or phrase) that could help realign your heart to him in those moments.

Pray

Lord, there is no God like you. When I feel overwhelmed by my circumstances, remind me of your greatness. When I am consumed by my weakness or weariness, turn my thoughts to praise. When I am tempted to give my attention to lesser things, pull my heart back to yours. Give me an undivided heart that I may honour you—now and for ever. Amen.

19

Only One Name

*"Salvation is found in no one else,
for there is no other name under heaven given to
mankind by which we must be saved."*

ACTS 4:12

Jesus is the only way to God.

How do you feel about that statement? I guess the answer may depend on who you are talking with. At church on Sundays, it is easy to sing this truth joyfully and with conviction. But in the workplace on Monday or when talking with unbelieving family members, it can be harder to declare it so unequivocally. Can there really be just one way for all eight billion people in the world to be saved?

But as I reflect on the uniqueness of God, it seems natural that there would also be one unique way to know him. In fact, given the *God*-ness of God, it is less surprising that there is one way and more astonishing that there is any way at all for us to know God and find rest in his presence. But when it comes to proclaiming salvation in Jesus alone, perhaps you sometimes feel more ashamed than awestruck. In Western society it is offensive to suggest there is one way to know or do anything—let alone to reach God. The 1st-century Roman world was no less pluralistic, and yet the apostle Peter is wonderfully unashamed of the truth that salvation is only possible through Jesus—because it is wonderfully good news!

Read Acts 4:1-12

The Jewish leaders are afraid of losing their religious and political power because men and women are responding to news of a God-man who rose from the dead and offers resurrection life to all who put their faith in him (v 2). Peter and John have spent a night in jail because of their teaching, but they are undeterred. They boldly proclaim the message of salvation through Jesus alone:

> *Salvation comes no other way; no other name has been or will be given to us by which we can be saved, only this one.*
> *(v 12, The Message)*

If you are familiar with this verse, it may not impact you in the way it would have struck Peter's original audience. So take some time to linger over it—and delight in what it means for you, personally.

Firstly, there is a way to be saved. The gap between God's purity and our impurity is enormous—but we have been given a way to enjoy a friendship and live in peace with him. This is incredible news! The sin that separates a holy God from unholy people does not have the final word in your life. Paradise is not lost to you for ever—there is a way back home.

Secondly, the way is wide open. It is not secret or hidden—you don't need to be clever enough to crack a code or privileged enough to receive a pass key. And it is not limited to people of a particular race, gender or social status. Jesus lived as a 1st-century Jewish man, but his name is given to *all* people as the name through which we are saved—male and female, Jew and Gentile, rich and poor. It is the name that has saved *you*. There is only one way to be saved—but the door is wide open and you have been welcomed through it. Praise God!

Lastly, salvation does not depend on you in any way. Jesus did everything necessary when he took the punishment for sin on himself. Only he could do it—because only he is the flawless Lamb; only he has the power to overcome the grave; only he is God. There was nothing you could do—and there is nothing you need to do! His name has been *given* to you—a name that promises "God saves". The angel told Joseph to "give him the name Jesus, because he will save his people from their sins". (Matthew 1:21)

In Jesus, God offers salvation for those who will believe. It is a generous gift that could never be bought or earned but is freely available to you. You never need to be ashamed of the gospel. It is liberating, life-giving news. Let Jesus—the way, the truth and the life—fill your heart with wonder and joy.

And everyone who calls
on the name of the L*ORD* *will be saved. (Joel 2:32)*

Cultivate

Could you share the wonderful news that salvation is found in Jesus alone with somebody you know? Anticipate some of their questions and think about how you might explain why this really is good news. Pray for an opportunity—and courage—to speak.

Pray

Use the words of Acts 4:12 to help you write a prayer of praise to Jesus.

20

Pierced by Joy

"You are worthy to take the scroll and to open its seals, because you were slain, and with your blood you purchased for God persons from every tribe and language and people and nation."

REVELATION 5:9

Towards the end of every great story is what Tolkien calls a "eucatastrophe". It's the unexpected about-turn that leads to a longed-for, but seemingly impossible, happy ending. In a letter to his son, he says the eucatastrophe "pierces you with a joy that brings tears … your whole nature … feels a sudden relief as if a major limb out of joint had suddenly snapped back"[3]. We feel this in *The Lord of the Rings* when Gandalf returns from the dead, as an even more powerful wizard than before. We sense all is not lost—the ring will be destroyed and peace will reign.

We've already peered over the apostle John's shoulder as he was given a behind-the-scenes vision of the throne room of heaven. We left with the elders' song ringing in our ears as they bowed before the throne in worship. But that extraordinary scene in Revelation 4 simply sets the stage for the drama to follow.

Read Revelation 5:1-14

In God's hand is a scroll with writing on both sides, sealed with seven seals. It seems that this scroll contains God's plan for the future, which John has been told he will be shown (Revelation 4:1). But no one in heaven or on earth can peek inside the scroll—or even open it! It isn't a matter of who might be strong enough to break the seals, but who is worthy—who has the right—to open the scroll and set God's plans in motion. If the scroll isn't opened, his purposes will not come to pass. No one will clean up the mess that humans have made of the world—there is no hope for us.

John is inconsolable. He has come close to seeing how God's plan for future redemption will unfold. But now, it seems, all is lost:

I wept and wept. (v 4)

I'm sure you sometimes feel a similar sense of despair when you look at the brokenness of our world. This yearning for restoration is something all of God's people experience—from the Fall all the way until the new creation. But we feel it most when life is painful. I imagine that John would have felt this deeply—he was an old man, exiled on an island used by the Romans as a labour camp. How his heart must have been strengthened by the vision of the heavenly throne room with its shimmering throne and joyful worshippers. How it must have broken moments later when the scroll could not be opened.

But then comes the eucatastrophe. When hope seems lost, a hero appears:

> *Do not weep! See, the Lion of the tribe of Judah, the Root of David, has triumphed. He is able to open the scroll and its seven seals.* (v 5)

There is a powerful King who has triumphed in battle and can open the scroll. But look closer—see the amazing twist in the tale:

> *Then I saw a Lamb, looking as if it had been slain.* (v 6)

The mighty Lion is a meek Lamb. He has been slaughtered, and he bears the wounds of weakness and shame. But now he is alive—risen from the dead! He stands at the centre of heaven's throne, his seven horns and seven eyes testifying to his total power and authority, wisdom and knowledge. His identity is clear: Jesus, the Lamb of God, who takes away the sin of the world! (John 1:29) He can take the scroll from the hand of God—and open the seven seals. As he does, heaven erupts in jubilant praise:

> *You are worthy to take the scroll*
> *and to open its seals,*
> *because you were slain,*
> *and with your blood you purchased for God*
> *persons from every tribe and language and people*
> *and nation.* (Revelation 5:9)

Jesus can open the scroll because he triumphed over sin, death and Satan—through the cross. With his blood he redeemed us from sin and its consequences, so that we belong to God. His death brings life, hope and a glorious future for "persons from every tribe and language and people and nation". No wonder countless angels—and every creature in heaven and earth—join in the praise!

Do you feel the power of the song? There is one living Lord. One triumphant King. The Lamb who was slain has defeated death and is enthroned in heaven. And one day, he will be enthroned on earth too. We are invited, with John, to *see* the Lamb on his throne. To exult in his victory. To delight in being part of his kingdom. To serve him as priests. To anticipate our future—reigning with him on a restored earth.

Cultivate

Take some time to reflect on the darkness, brokenness and groaning of our world. Don't rush—let yourself sit with it for a few minutes. (If it helps, you could turn off the lights.) Then read Revelation 5 again.

Listen to "Is He Worthy?" By Andrew Peterson. Sing (or shout!) the answer to each question: *We do; it is; he does; he is!*

Pray

Worthy is the Lamb, who was slain,
to receive power and wealth and wisdom and strength
and honour and glory and praise!

His Greatness

TRUSTING IN GOD'S RULE

21

Unshakeable

"He will be the sure foundation for your times."

ISAIAH 33:6

My son was three weeks old when an earthquake in the Indian Ocean caused a giant tsunami that ravaged the coastal communities of Indonesia, Thailand, India and several other countries around the Indian Ocean. Holding my tiny newborn in my arms, I watched with horror as television news reports showed chaos, destruction and devastating loss of life. No one saw it coming. No one was prepared. No one could have prevented it. It seems we are all vulnerable to disruption and upheaval, hurt and harm—from the smallest and weakest to the wisest and greatest. Tragedy does not discriminate.

Everyone longs for stability. We all want life to be unshaken and unshakeable. It's a built-in ache in our souls, this yearning to be secure. But from a human perspective, it seems a futile desire. Even if we are fortunate enough to live in relative peace, we know life can be turned upside down in an instant. With one phone call, one conversation, one disastrous blow. An unexpected diagnosis. A relationship break-up. Redundancy. Repossession. Global tragedy.

And yet, there is a promise of stability and security for those who fear the Lord.

Read Isaiah 33:2-6, 17-22

The people of Judah are vulnerable—and they know it. Assyria, the world superpower, has conquered neighbouring Samaria and continues to threaten Judah despite having been paid to withdraw their attacks (2 Kings 18). The king of Assyria rules through terror and corruption. Everyone is living in fear of him.

But although Judah may experience distress and unrest, Isaiah prophesies that the Lord "will be the sure foundation for [their] times, a rich store of salvation and wisdom and knowledge" (v 6). He is unshakeable and will keep them secure. He will provide them with an abundance of salvation, wisdom and knowledge—all they need to live as his people. When they long for stability, they need only look to him.

This promise is also true for you and I. You may not feel vulnerable to threats of siege, famine or war (although women in many countries are), but I imagine you feel unsettled, unstable and fearful at times. You ache for peace and stability, an end to turmoil and toil. The wonderful promise of Isaiah 33:6 is that the Lord is the firm and steady foundation on which every day of your life rests secure.

Jesus encourages his followers with this same truth in his Sermon on the Mount (Matthew 7:24-25). He says that those who hear and obey his words are as secure as a house built on an immovable rock. Even though wild winds beat against that house and turbulent tides rise around it, it will not fall because its foundation is secure.

One of the realities of living this side of eternity is that life may not always appear secure, but this truth still stands. We have stability in knowing that Jesus has conquered our greatest enemies of sin and death through his death and resurrection, and that our heavenly Father is working all things together for our good (Romans 8:28). But there is even greater stability to come when Jesus returns and Zion—the place where God's people will live with him—is filled with justice and righteousness. You may feel the winds beating against the walls of your life right now, but in the new creation you will experience no vulnerability. No violence. No terror or corruption. Your eyes will see King Jesus in his beauty, and you will never feel unstable again.

Cultivate

List some of the things that make you feel unstable or insecure. How does remembering that the Lord is your sure foundation help you view these things differently? How will each one be different in the new creation?

Pray

I praise you, Father, that you are the sure foundation for my times. Thank you that I don't need to feel insecure because you are the rock beneath my feet that cannot be moved or shaken. You provide your people with a rich store of salvation, wisdom and knowledge—all we need in every situation. You are working all things together for my good, and you will lead me home to the new creation where justice and righteousness will dwell for ever. Please increase my trust and confidence in you as I wait for that day. Amen.

22

When Oceans Roar

"Your throne was established long ago;
you are from all eternity."

PSALM 93:2

I doubt many people alive today have heard of Sargon the Great. Around 2334 BC, he conquered most of ancient Mesopotamia (modern-day Iraq) and the surrounding region, and established what is thought to be the oldest empire in the world—the Akkadian Empire. But despite Sargon's long reign, impressive military accomplishments and powerful dynasty, he eventually died. Both his sons were assassinated, and the whole empire collapsed by 2083 BC—less than 300 years after it was founded.

But the reign of our Lord is eternal. There was no king before him and there will be no king after him—his kingdom is everlasting.

Read Psalm 93

This little psalm tells us everything we need to know about the rule of God: *The Lord reigns!* The psalmist isn't reading this from a script in a monotone; he's shouting it joyfully as a declaration of victory! The psalmist celebrates with exuberance in the Lord's kingship and rejoices in his strength. I love the picture of the Lord being robed in majesty and armed with strength (v 1). It's as though the psalmist is saying, *Wherever the Lord goes, majesty and strength go too.* The Lord is draped in majesty and covered in strength—they are inseparable from him.

When I started teaching, a more experienced teacher told me, "If you want your pupils to listen and learn, you need to be the biggest character in the room". I don't know whether I always managed that (or even if it mattered), but we can be sure that the Lord is always the most majestic being in every room. We can also be sure that, unlike the Akkadian Empire, his kingdom will never collapse. Why? Because it was established from the beginning of time (v 2, CSB). It has endured from eternity past and will endure into eternity future. The statutes—or laws—of this kingdom are completely reliable and can't be changed (v 5). The Lord's reign will be holy—for ever!

Your statutes, LORD, stand firm;
holiness adorns your house
for endless days. (v 5)

Even among the greatest, wisest and most compassionate world leaders, none rule with absolute holiness all the time. All fail to live up to their inauguration promises in some way. It is inevitable, because they are only human and finite. But the Lord is eternally holy, which means that when turbulent waters rise and threaten to overwhelm, we can be confident that he will always rule perfectly and with absolute purity.

The poetic style of verse 3 gives an impression of increasing danger as the lines repeat and build on one another. The "seas" or "floods" lift up their voices in anger and threaten to destroy with their pounding waves. If you've ever watched an ocean disaster movie you can probably picture a boat tossed uncontrollably around the ocean as waters rise higher and higher and waves beat louder and louder against the hull. Whether the psalmist envisioned a danger or threat arising to God's people, or whether he is just comparing God's might against the crashing powers of the waves, verse 4 offers immediate assurance that the Lord is mightier still. In the Bible, the seas often represent chaos and destruction. But these turbulent waters that cannot be contained by human efforts are no match for him. He is not overwhelmed by the whelming floods.

You and I can face each day with confidence—knowing that the Lord is in perfect and eternal control. We can sleep in peace each night—knowing that he will still be reigning in the morning. He will never die and his kingdom won't be overthrown. His reign is holy—for ever and ever.

Cultivate

Listen to "The Lord Almighty Reigns (Psalm 93)" by Sovereign Grace.

Write verses 1 and 5 of this psalm on little cards and keep them in your bag or set them as reminders on your phone. The next time you feel dismayed by the unrest and terror caused by ungodly rulers, read them out loud and remind your soul that the Lord is the only true and eternal ruler—and his rule is righteous and holy.

Pray

Lord, you are mightier than the mighty waters, stronger than the surging seas. You reign when oceans roar and tides rise. You reign amidst the floods. You reign above the storms of life. You are from everlasting to everlasting. And you are holy and just in all your ways. Faithful God, you are worthy of all my praise. Please help me to trust you, whatever this week brings. Amen.

23

True Wisdom

"To God belong wisdom and power;
counsel and understanding are his."

JOB 12:13

A few years ago, I was deeply discouraged by some relational conflict I was experiencing with someone who I needed to work closely with. As I offloaded my frustrations and fears to a friend, he listened carefully. He skilfully diagnosed the issues at the heart of the conflict and offered wise suggestions for moving forward—helping me understand what could be resolved and what I needed to accept and learn to handle more patiently and compassionately. I am so grateful to have a friend I can rely on for such insight and understanding. Over the years, I have often felt in awe of his wisdom—and I would like to grow in this attribute myself. (My friend is quite a bit older than me, so I am hopeful there is time!)

I imagine Job would have appreciated a friend like mine. In Job 12, he rebukes his three unwise friends for their unfair accusations about him and their wrong thinking about God. These "comforters" believe they know far more than Job.

They seek to explain and justify the terrible suffering Job is experiencing. They think they know what God is doing—and what Job must do if he wants his suffering to end. Job responds by showing that only God is truly wise. Only he has complete understanding and perfect insight.

Read Job 12:13-22

Job's knowledge of God's wisdom enables him to persevere in suffering and withstand the discouragement of ungodly friends. While he has questions about his own situation, he doesn't doubt it is God who is in control and who knows all things. In verse 13, he offers a clear statement about the Lord's sovereignty—over his life and over the whole world. Job is not on a quest for a source of wisdom and power—he already knows exactly where they are located:

True wisdom and power are found in God;
counsel and understanding are his. (v 13, NLT)

I don't know about you, but I am often slow to remember this. When I don't know what is going on or what I should do, I scrabble around looking for a friend or counsellor to guide me. I forget that I can go straight to the source of wisdom himself. Don't mishear me: the Lord does graciously impart wisdom and guidance through others—especially within the church. But we need to acknowledge that any wisdom we or our friends may have is ultimately from him. He is the one to whom wisdom and understanding belong.

Did you notice how Job links the Lord's wisdom and strength in verses 13 and 16? Unlike us, the Lord always knows what to do—and also has the power to do it. Isn't this reassuring? If he were wise but not powerful, that would be of little comfort—he wouldn't necessarily be able to use his wisdom to do what is good and right. If he were powerful but not wise, we could not be confident that he would always use his power in the right way. But this combination assures us that he can and will always do what is right and best. We cannot have that same confidence in anyone else.

As I pause now to thank God for my friend and the times his wisdom has been a help and encouragement to me, I am mindful that the Lord's wisdom is worthy of so much more praise. Who else could conceive of a way to lovingly redeem a broken world and rescue condemned sinners from judgment? And to achieve all of it without compromising his justice or betraying his righteousness? Who else would choose to showcase his wisdom to the rulers and authorities in the heavenly realms through the church? We can worship together with the apostle Paul:

Oh, the depth of the riches
and the wisdom and the knowledge of God!
How unsearchable his judgments
and untraceable his ways! (Romans 11:33, CSB)

Cultivate

Where do you typically look for wisdom? Are there times you run to other people (in real life or online) before turning to the Lord? Try to establish a habit of coming to him first—acknowledging that wisdom and understanding belong to him, and asking him to guide you. (He may well prompt you to talk with a friend, family member or ministry leader, but be sure to talk to him first!)

Pray

Lord, you are the source of all wisdom. You are the only one who is perfect in knowledge and understanding. Forgive me that I often search for wisdom in other places rather than coming straight to you. Thank you that I can always trust you to know exactly what to do—and, in your wise timing, to do it. Please increase my confidence in you and help me run to you when I lack wisdom myself. Amen.

24

Coming on the Clouds

"His dominion is an everlasting dominion
that will not pass away,
and his kingdom is one that will never be destroyed."

DANIEL 7:14

Around 550 years before Jesus was born, a man named Daniel had a terrifying dream. He was given a startling glimpse into the spiritual realm, and it left him troubled.

Read Daniel 7:1-14

Daniel sees a giant windstorm, churning up the sea. Four strange animals rise out of the waters. One looks like a lion but with eagle's wings and a human mind. One is like a ferocious bear with three ribs in its mouth. One looks like a leopard, but it has four wings on its back and four heads. The fourth creature is the most terrifying of all with its huge iron teeth and ten horns. It crushes and devours its victims. Three of its horns are displaced by a little horn that sprouts up in front of Daniel with eyes like a human and a boastful mouth. It is horrifying.

As the dream continues, thrones appear, and the "Ancient of Days" enters what looks like a heavenly courtroom and takes his seat as judge of all the earth. He is awesome looking, with white robes, hair like wool and a fiery throne with blazing wheels and a river of fire flowing from his presence. It is like nothing on earth. Books are opened in front of him and the beasts are judged according to their evil deeds. The first three are stripped of their authority, and the fourth is silenced for ever and destroyed in the blazing fire.

The dream then takes an unexpected turn with the arrival of "one like a son of man, coming with the clouds of heaven" (v 13). He approaches the Ancient of Days who gives him "authority, glory and sovereign power." He is human, but rides on the clouds like God himself (Psalm 104:3). He is given an everlasting dominion and a kingdom that will never be destroyed. People from every nation worship him.

It is not hard to work out who this is. Daniel is being given a preview of the risen and ascended Lord Jesus entering heaven's throne room, having disarmed and disgraced the spiritual rulers and authorities through the cross (Colossians 2:15). Jesus describes himself like this when he testifies to the high priest after his arrest:

> *And you will see the Son of Man sitting at the right hand of the Mighty One and coming on the clouds of heaven.*
> *(Mark 14:62)*

At this point, Jesus is about to be killed, but he knows that his death and resurrection will lead to exaltation, glory and a kingdom that will endure for ever. This is the turning point in human history—the fulfilment of God's promise of a snake-crusher who will reverse the curse and redeem his people (Genesis 3:15). And it's so certain to happen that Daniel is given a picture of it over 500 years beforehand!

The beasts in the dream represent four kings—or empires—that will rise from the earth (Daniel 7:3, 17). The first is most likely Babylon, where Daniel is living. The identity of the other three is less certain—perhaps they represent the Medo-Persian, Greek and Roman Empires or maybe various kingdoms throughout history that have opposed God. What is certain is the intensifying evil and terror they bring against God's people.

But although the beasts are terrifying, they will not triumph. They will oppose God, but they will not succeed in overthrowing his kingdom. He sees the kingdoms that stand against him and terrorise his people—and he will judge. Only he has the right to judge all the kingdoms and people of the world because only he has been there from the beginning—the Ancient of Days. He will silence the beasts and destroy their power:

> *But the holy people of the Most High will receive the kingdom and will possess it for ever—yes, for ever and ever.*
> *(v 18)*

God's people are safe—even from the terror of the beasts. Jesus has won the victory over every evil power and has already begun his reign as sovereign King of every nation and people. All authority has been given to him, and those who continue to stand against him will ultimately be destroyed. But those who belong to the Most High will reign with him for eternity.

Cultivate

Imagine Jesus, riding into heaven's throne room on the clouds, approaching the throne and being given authority over every other ruler. Remind yourself that the fourth beast has been destroyed—and the others are on a short leash. Let this heavenly perspective fill your heart with amazement and hope when it seems that those who oppose God are winning.

Pray

Write a prayer praising Jesus for his victory over evil and his rule as King of the nations. Ask him to help you wait patiently for his return.

25

Exalted For Ever

"Great is the Lord and most worthy of praise;
his greatness no one can fathom."

PSALM 145:3

As I read the Old Testament, one of the things I love about King David is his unabashed, unrestrained praise of God. David wasn't a flawless leader by any means (think Bathsheba, Uriah, Tamar…), but he loved the Lord, and his love spilled over into joyful and enthusiastic declarations of praise and wonder. One example of this is Psalm 145.

Read Psalm 145

This psalm is both a song *of* praise and a song *about* praise. David delights in God himself—but also in the praise that God will receive as his people exalt, praise, extol, commend, tell, speak, meditate, proclaim, celebrate, sing and make known his worth and his works. He knows it is right that those who have experienced God's goodness, greatness and glory make a noise about it!

A couple of years ago I enjoyed the nicest ice cream I have ever eaten—and I have not stopped talking about it! All my friends (and plenty of others) now know about the little shop in Oxford that makes the best hazelnut ice cream in the world—and some of them have been dragged there to sample the goodness for themselves. I am embarrassed to say I have not always proclaimed the greatness of God with as much enthusiasm—and I imagine I am not alone in that.

I think the reason is that, at various points in my Christian life, I have lost my wonder. The hazelnut ice cream in Oxford blew me away because I'm not usually bothered about ice cream, and I wasn't expecting it to taste so incredible. It awakened new feelings of delight that I then needed to share.

When we read God's word and discover how wonderful he is, it surprises and delights us too. But if we are not careful to keep spending time with him and reflecting on his greatness, we will lose that first spark of wonder and become complacent in our worship. I think David knew this. Yes, this psalm is the natural response of a heart devoted to the Lord. But it also shows a conscious choice to love him more:

I will exalt you, my God the King;
I will praise your name for ever and ever.
Every day I will praise you
and extol your name for ever and ever. (v 1-2)

His words are emphatic: he *will* praise and exalt God every single day of his life. We need to do this too if we do not want our awe of God to diminish. Even when we can't honestly say we feel a sense of awe, when we choose to focus on the Lord and bring him praise, the Spirit tunes our hearts to him—and our feelings eventually catch up.

There's an old saying, "What grips your heart wags your tongue". Of course, as we saw from Daniel 7, the obvious response is worship. But I find that as I grow in awe of God, my response is not only vertical—that is, directed to him. It is also horizontal—directed to others. When our hearts become captivated by him, as we meditate on the wonderful works of God, our tongues will wag and we will not be able to stop ourselves from speaking about his kingdom and might, "so that all people may know of [his] mighty acts and the glorious splendour of [his] kingdom." (v 12).

Verse 4 of the psalm implies that this is the main way that the gospel will spread through generations:

One generation commends your works to another;
they tell of your mighty acts.

Evangelism can sometimes feel like an overwhelming task, but it doesn't always have to be complicated. As God's people (you and me) are blown away by his greatness and glory, our mouths will overflow with praise—and future generations will come to know him too!

Cultivate

Spend some time this week meditating on God's wonderful works (v 5). Write down some of the ways he is greater than anything or anyone else—keep going until you are overcome by his greatness. Let your delight in him spill over by sharing what astounds you about him with a friend or family member.

Pray

Lord, you are great and most worthy of praise. I cannot fully comprehend your greatness, but I ask you to help me grasp it more and more. Help me never lose my wonder but continue to amaze me as I meditate on your wonderful works. Please let my heart be captivated and enthralled by you, and loosen my tongue to speak of your power, commend your works, and proclaim your great deeds—so that others may know you too. Amen.

His Kindness

TREASURING GOD'S MERCY

26

Depths of Compassion

"Who is a God like you, who pardons sin…?"

MICAH 7:18A

What do you do when faced with the stark reality of your sin? Shrug off those thoughts as too painful to deal with? Overanalyse and tie yourself up in knots about failure? When we come face-to-face with our weakness and guilt, what we most need is to look more intently into the unchanging character of our God. In particular, to meditate on his mercy.

Read Micah 7:18-20

These verses of hope and forgiveness follow after several prophecies about God's justice and judgment. Micah prophesied to the people of Judah around 700 years before Jesus was born, warning them that God's judgment was coming on those who disregard his law and dishonour his people. God's justice means he cares deeply about wrongdoing and cannot simply overlook sin—it must be punished. But there is a wonderful reassurance for those who belong to him.

You do not stay angry for ever
but delight to show mercy.
You will again have compassion on us;
you will tread our sins underfoot
and hurl all our iniquities into the depths of the sea.
(v 18b-19)

God isn't reluctant to forgive our sin. He doesn't do so in weary resignation, eye-rolling because we have messed up again. Rather, it brings him great joy to show us mercy. I love the Message paraphrase of the end of verse 18:

You don't nurse your anger and don't stay angry long,
for mercy is your specialty. That's what you love most.

Mercy is his speciality! Our God is an expert in mercy—he never tires of showing kindness to those who look to him. His compassion is inexhaustible.

I was eleven when I first realised that I was a sinner and couldn't save myself. I confessed my need of God's mercy and trusted in the death of Jesus to atone for my sin. I knew straightaway that I was forgiven for ever. What I didn't understand then is that the gospel is not only for those who need to come to Christ for the first time. It is for all of us—every day.

While forgiveness is instant, sanctification (the process of becoming holy) takes a lifetime. We continue to sin every day, so we need God's mercy and forgiveness every day. The wonderful news is that God does not tire of our struggle with sin but delights to show mercy—over and over and over again. He doesn't keep track of how many times we need to come to him for forgiveness. He throws our sins into the deepest part of the sea—and like a heavy boulder, they sink to the bottom, never to be seen again. Picture a deep, swirling sea and imagine accidentally dropping your phone or a precious piece of jewellery into it. You'd be horrified, knowing that it's lost for ever. But with our sins, it is wonderful to know that they are lost to the depths of the sea for ever—never to be recovered and held against us!

Do you ever confess your sins to the Lord—but then replay them over and over again in your mind? It is natural to continue to feel regret over wrong things we have said and done—especially when they have caused harm to others. But you don't need to carry a burden of guilt and shame on your shoulders. When Jesus died on the cross, he bore the weight of all your sin and guilt and shame—so you don't have to! Our God has promised to faithfully love us from "days long ago" (v 20) and he continues to do so despite all our unfaithfulness. The depths of his mercy are deeper than the deepest sea.

Cultivate

The next time you feel overwhelmed by guilt or shame over sin that you have already confessed and repented of, imagine that sin falling into the swirling deep sea and declare to your soul, "Yes, I am a sinner and I deserve judgment. But the Lord has hurled all my sins into the depths of the sea—and they are gone for ever. I will not go searching for them but will rejoice in his infinite mercy."

Pray

Father, thank you that your mercy is so much greater than all my sin. Thank you that you do not tire of forgiving but delight to show mercy. Thank you that you do not keep a record of wrongs but have removed my sins from your sight—never to be brought up again! When I am weighed down by guilt and shame, please help me remember your mercy. And when I am tempted to gloss over my sin, please give me faith to come to you in repentance, knowing that you are ready to forgive. Amen.

27

A Show like No Other

"...so that in the coming ages he might display the immeasurable riches of his grace through his kindness to us in Christ Jesus."

EPHESIANS 2:7, CSB

Why are you a Christian?

I don't mean, what do you believe makes you a Christian. Or, what attracted you to accept God's offer of life in Christ. I'm asking, what is God's great, eternal goal in saving you? What is his great, eternal goal in saving me?

We'll come back to this. But first, let's remind ourselves why we needed saving in the first place. In his letter to the 1st-century church in Ephesus, the apostle Paul offers a succinct yet comprehensive summary of our condition before and after conversion.

Read Ephesians 2:1-10

If we are ever tempted to think we were not *that* bad before God intervened, Paul sets us straight. He describes our former state as dead! It isn't that we were struggling to get it together or just missing the mark or not quite able to attain God's standards for holiness. No, Paul says that, spiritually speaking, we weren't even conscious. We were corpses—crumbling and decaying in the dirt. Unable to save ourselves, and undeserving of rescue from our helpless, hopeless state.

But God...

God is so rich in mercy and so full of love that he made us alive. This is all grace. There was no hint of goodness in us—no redeemable quality worth paying for. But "because of his great love for us" God disrupted our deadness, raised us to life and seated us with his Son in the heavenly realms. What incomparable kindness! What indescribable love!

But while this explains *how* we were saved, it doesn't fully answer the question, *why?* Paul gets to the *why* in verse 7:

> *So that in the coming ages he might display the immeasurable riches of his grace through his kindness to us in Christ Jesus. (CSB)*

God wants us to know him as he really is—supremely great, gloriously holy, immensely powerful and infinitely wise. He also wants us to know that he is *immeasurably* gracious and kind. He is mighty *and* merciful. Great *and* full of grace. And he wants us to relate to him as a kind and gracious Father.

The reason that our unspeakably great God condescended to rescue, raise and redeem spiritually dead people like you and me is because he wants to show the riches of his grace and kindness to us—and because they are immeasurable, it will take eternity to do so!

God's purposes for our salvation are not limited to this present world. Only eternity is long enough to showcase the riches of his grace. They will never run out. We will explore the riches of God's kindness throughout the "coming ages"—

and we won't get bored! He will continue to astound and amaze us with discovery after discovery of his grace. And after a few billion years, we will still be scratching the surface of all there is to know!

God's ultimate purpose in saving you and I is to showcase his kindness—and it is a show like no other. My parents lived in Florida for a while, and when my children were small, we flew out to visit them. They bought tickets to Disney World and we got to experience the nightly firework displays at the Magic Kingdom and EPCOT. They were unlike any other firework shows we had seen. Music played, fireworks dazzled, fountains danced, and the crowd was spellbound by spectacular displays that seemed to go on and on, surprising and delighting us with every twist and turn. My children were mesmerised—and so was I! But this is nothing compared to the display of God's kindness that we will experience throughout eternity. The never-ending, breath-taking, extravagant riches of his grace will astonish and delight us like nothing else could.

Eternity will be exhilarating. God will continue to reveal more and more of his kindness—and our capacity to enjoy him will grow and grow. This is God's ultimate goal in saving you and me. And it is only possible through Jesus. It is *in Christ* that God has expressed his kindness to us. Only in him can we receive and experience the grace of God. Only through him can the dead receive life. In Christ, God shows the immeasurable riches of his compassion. In Christ, he gets all the glory—and we get to share his joy.

Cultivate

Share Ephesians 2:4-7 with a friend this week. Marvel together over the immeasurable riches of God's kindness and how thrilling it will be to spend eternity discovering more and more of them.

Pray

Father, I can't begin to imagine how wonderful it will be to spend eternity exploring and marvelling at the incomparable riches of your grace. I am already awed by the kindness you have shown me in the Lord Jesus—it is incredible to know that there is so much more for me to discover. Thank you for saving me. Thank you for rescuing me from death and giving me life—only you could do that. Thank you for my certain hope of eternity with you. Amen.

28

Mercy Meets Us

"Because of the LORD's great love we are not consumed, for his compassions never fail."

LAMENTATIONS 3:22

Jerusalem had been under siege for over a year and a half when the Babylonian army finally broke through its walls and set fire to the temple, the royal palace and all the houses and important buildings (2 Kings 25). The city was devastated, its inhabitants slaughtered. The temple and palace treasures were carried off to Babylon—along with anyone who had escaped starvation or the sword. Only the poorest in the land were left behind to work the vineyards and fields. It was a time of unimaginable horror for God's people.

One survivor records the overwhelming sorrow and distress suffered during the siege and destruction of Jerusalem in a collection of poems. They are dark, raw expressions of grief and despair—and they made it into the Old Testament.

Isn't the Lord kind to include poems and songs of lament in his word? Sometimes we need to "borrow" language to express our grief when our own words seem insufficient. While you or I may never experience the horrors of siege, starvation and exile, we will certainly suffer in some way. During these times of suffering, we may have questions about God's character and his commitment to us. The laments of Scripture remind us that we are not the first people to ask these questions.

In Lamentations, the poet expresses his sorrow over the devastation of Jerusalem. His soul is in turmoil as he recalls the affliction of God's people. He knows it is brought about by their disobedience of God's law and refusal to listen to his prophets (Deuteronomy 28:47-57; Amos 2:4-5)—and that makes the suffering even more bitter. But there is a glimmer of hope in the middle of his laments as the poet remembers not only his affliction but also the Lord's unfailing love and compassion.

Read Lamentations 3:1-9, 19-24

"Yet this I call to mind ..."

In the midst of misery, the poet remembers mercy—and it gives him hope. This does not spring from a change in circumstances or the counsel of a friend but from the character of his God.

It is the Lord's love and compassion that bring hope. The knowledge that his love is not fickle or flaky like human love so often is, but it is faithful and firm. The promise that his mercies never run out but are new every morning. The poet doesn't need to worry about using up his quota of mercy on a particularly bad day—because the Lord has an unending supply! As surely as the sun will rise, so the Lord's compassion will rise to meet him.

And so it will rise to meet us. Whatever trouble we face, whatever dark night of the soul we go through, the Lord's kindness will meet us there. It is a given. We can rely on it—like oxygen for our lungs and gravity for our feet. The day will break. The sun will rise. The Lord's compassion will meet us in the morning. His faithfulness is so great that there is no risk in trusting him to show up with new mercies—every day of our lives!

> *Great is his faithfulness;*
> *his mercies begin afresh each morning. (v 23, NLT)*

Do you need to call to mind the Lord's love and compassion today? Perhaps you experience chronic pain or frequent migraines, debilitating anxiety, loneliness or depression. Maybe you are recently widowed or grieving the loss of a dear friend. Maybe you are waiting for a job offer, a place to live, or a medical diagnosis—or hoping for reconciliation with a loved one. Perhaps you are consumed by anger, resentment, envy or bitterness. In your suffering or struggle, will you call to mind the Lord's unfailing compassion towards you? Will you trust him to be faithful to his character and his word? Will you choose to believe that his mercies will meet *you* each day? Will you say, with the poet, "The Lord is my portion; therefore I will wait for him"?

Cultivate

Listen to "As Sure as the Sun" by Ellie Holcomb.

List some ways you have experienced God's kindness in times of difficulty or pain. How might recalling his kindness to you in the past encourage you to look for evidence of his kindness in the present?

Pray

Lord, you are a good and kind God. Your love is faithful and your compassions never fail—they are new every morning. Your mercy meets me each morning and continues with me through the watches of the night. Thank you that I can look back over my life and trace your kindness, even through difficult times. Help me to rejoice in your kindness every day—even when my circumstances are not what I would choose. Amen.

29

Kindness Came

"But when the kindness and love of God our Saviour appeared, he saved us."

TITUS 3:4-5

I don't know about you, but God's kindness is the attribute I feel most able to relate to. Although imperfectly and inconsistently, I can reflect God's kindness in a way that is simply impossible with other attributes like glory or greatness. Kindness is what theologians call a "communicable" attribute—something that is true of God and can also be true of us. But while kindness is a quality we can mirror to some degree in our human relationships, God's kindness extends far beyond what we can imagine or imitate.

Theologian and pastor A.W. Tozer says, "God is a God of utter kindness and cordiality and good will and benevolence". God does not only show kindness; he *is* kindness. It is what he is like all the time. He is never mean, resentful or cruel. He is never grumpy, bad-tempered or aloof. We see this in the stories of Old Testament women like Sarah, Hagar, Leah, Rahab, Ruth, Hannah and Abigail. We see it today as he causes the sun to shine and rain to fall, and gives us air to breathe. He is kind to those who believe in him, and to those who don't, to those who are evil and to those who are good (Matthew 5:45). And in kindness, he saved us.

Read Titus 3:3-7

The full extent of God's kindness is shown in Christ. The kindness of God entered our world, wrapped in flesh, bringing life and hope. In the Gospels we see Jesus cuddling little children and comforting grieving mothers. We see him feeding the hungry and healing the sick. We see him pursuing people no one else wanted anything to do with—tax collectors, lepers, Samaritans, outcasts and misfits. The kind of people you and I might turn away from. We see him giving his life to save those who couldn't save themselves—people like you and me.

When we were "foolish, disobedient, deceived, enslaved by various passions and pleasures, living in malice and envy, hateful, detesting one another" (v 3, CSB), God did not retreat in discouragement, disgust or despair. Instead, he ran towards us.

When someone hurts me or treats me unfairly, I want to retreat—usually in an effort to protect myself from further pain. I can do the same with people whose viewpoints or behaviour I find offensive. It feels too frustrating, discouraging or energy-consuming to try to engage. It is easier to pull away. But God did not disengage when we rejected and betrayed him. Instead, he came close. He sacrificed himself, gave us life and poured his Spirit into our lives. His kindness led to our rescue, our renewal and an unbreakable relationship with him.

We tend to think of kindness as a "soft" quality: someone is considered kind if they are even-tempered, undemanding, sensitive and gentle. God is gentle with us, but his kindness is also strong, compelling and transformative. It doesn't leave us as it finds us, but draws us into a richer, fuller way of life. I love how Eugene Peterson puts it in The Message:

> *God is kind, but he's not soft. In kindness he takes us firmly by the hand and leads us into a radical life-change.*
>
> *(Romans 2:4, The Message)*

God's kindness in Jesus frees us from slavery to sin and changes our desires so they reflect his. It teaches us to say no to ungodliness, and to live with wisdom, righteousness and devotion to God (Titus 2:12). It also shapes the way we respond to others. When we remember how undeserving we were of God's salvation, we are more able to forgive people who hurt us and bear with those who are unlike us.

God's kindness is ultimately seen at the cross. The kindness of God hung bleeding and dying so that you and I need never go a day without knowing we are loved and accepted. Jesus suffered humiliation so that we may be free from shame. He relinquished his right to glory so that we can one day share in it with him (Romans 8:17).

Cultivate

Think about someone you find it hard to show kindness to. How might you approach conversations with that person differently as you remember God's kindness to you in Christ?

Pray

Lord Jesus, you are more worthy of my praise than I can express. I deserved wrath but you came running towards me in kindness and love. I was a slave to sin but you rescued me and turned my life around. I praise you for your wonderful gift of life. I praise you for forgiveness, freedom and the promise of future glory with you. As I reflect on your kindness to me, please work in my heart so that I may reflect it to those around me—for your glory alone. Amen.

30

An Invitation

"He has shown you, O mortal, what is good. And what does the Lord require of you? To act justly and to love mercy and to walk humbly with your God."

MICAH 6:8

Worship is …

How would you complete that sentence?

For ancient Jews, worship of the Lord was expressed primarily through sacrificial offerings. Rams and goats, bulls and calves, doves and pigeons; crops and bread; olive oil, wine and incense were all offered at the altar—to atone for sin, and as expressions of thankfulness and dedication to him. But it was possible to perform these sacrifices and still fall short of the worship God requires.

Read Micah 6:6-8

In verses 6 and 7, Micah suggests some potentially appropriate responses to the kindness of God in rescuing his people. Should they come before the Lord with the costly sacrifice of year-old calves? Would the Lord be pleased with more extravagant offerings—thousands of rams and an ocean of olive oil? Should they even consider a human sacrifice? (It sounds crazy, but one of the kings who reigned during Micah's time did just that—see 2 Kings 16:2-3.)

But then he reminds the people that the Lord is less interested in outward, showy displays of worship than in a faithful life.

And what does the Lord require of you?
To act justly and to love mercy
and to walk humbly with your God. (Micah 6:8)

Growing in awe of God leads to deeper delight in his character, more gratitude for his grace, and an insatiable longing to know him more. I have started to experience this as I have reflected on the attributes of God we have looked at together. As I consider how this may impact my day-to-day life going forward, I anticipate a richer prayer life, deeper devotion to the Lord, and greater joy in living for him. But Micah's words are a challenging reminder that awe of God also results in kindness to others.

God acts justly—so we should too. God loves mercy—so we should love it too. These are personal commands that require a personal response. And they are as costly as the sacrifices of bulls and rams because they go against the grain of our nature.

Acting justly is about more than avoiding unjust behaviour or ensuring that acts of injustice are punished. God cares deeply for the weak and vulnerable, and he is committed to doing what is good for them. To act justly is to reflect him in that desire. Loving mercy (or kindness, ESV) means more than performing random acts of kindness now and again. God is devoted to mercy—he delights in loving and serving those who have nothing to offer in return.

The Hebrew word used for mercy is *hesed*. It is used throughout the Old Testament to describe God's unlimited, unwavering loving-kindness for his people. It is not dutiful but delights to serve. It is not fickle or fluctuating but firm and faithful. Its perfect fulfilment is at the cross where God gave his Son as the atoning sacrifice for our sins (1 John 4:10).

If I am honest, I like the idea of *hesed* love more than the practice of it. I feel a bit overwhelmed by the call to reflect God's mercy and kindness to other people. It is costly—and it can seem impossible. The good news is that God has given us new hearts that are able to love in ways that are costly and counterintuitive. We can read Micah 6:8 not as words of condemnation but of invitation.

As we have worked through these devotions together, I have encouraged us to look up. To take our eyes off ourselves and our circumstances, and fix them on the Lord who is so much greater. But as we look up to him, he also encourages us to look out. He invites us to respond to his greatness and glory not only by delighting in him but also by delighting to serve others.

Does this seem an obvious response to the "exalted God" we have considered? You might expect him to require public declarations of devotion, extended times of prayer or a greater commitment to mission. But while these are not inappropriate responses, what he's after is a life of continual closeness with him and an ongoing commitment to reflect him in our relationships with others. It's both a liberating and exciting invitation. How will you respond?

Cultivate

Take some time to consider how you will continue to cultivate awe going forward. Think of some small habits you could build into your daily or weekly rhythms that will encourage you to reflect on the characteristics of God we have looked at. Plan some regular times to offer prayers of praise as well as petition. Invite a friend to check on how you are growing in awe (maybe monthly).

Pray

Write a prayer of response:

- Start by focusing on God's character and what he has shown you about himself through these devotions. Take time to delight in each attribute.
- Thank him for some specific ways these attributes impact your life personally.
- Ask him to continue to reveal more of his God-ness and ask that you will continue to grow in awe each day

Acknowledgements

My wonderful editor, Catherine Bernard: I am thankful for your wisdom, insight and constant encouragement throughout this project. The book is so much better because of you.

The team at The Good Book Company: you are a blessing to the church, and it's a joy to serve with you. Katy Morgan: thank you especially for your invaluable help in the early stages of this project.

I am thankful for the many friends who have prayed for me and cheered me on as I have worked on this book. I am especially grateful for my ministry colleagues and church leaders, who are such an encouragement.

My family, who love me so well and help me love Jesus more: each of you teach me more about our amazing God—Richard, through your steadfastness and unconditional love; Tiana, through your compassion and servant heart; Jed, through your concern for justice and passion for the lost. Thanks for all you are and do!

Our awesome God:

> *Praise and glory and wisdom and thanks and honour and power and strength be to [you] for ever and ever. Amen!*
>
> *(Revelation 7:12)*

Journal

GROWING IN AWE OF GOD

Amazed

Endnotes

1 C.S. Lewis, *Mere Christianity* (Fontana Books, 1970), p. 108.

2 Martin Luther, *Summaries*. Quoted by Christopher Ash, *The Psalms: a Christ-Centered Commentary* (Crossway, 2024), p. 464.

3 J.R.R Tolkien, *The Letters of J. R. R. Tolkien* (Allen & Unwin, 1981), p. 100.

BIBLICAL | RELEVANT | ACCESSIBLE

At The Good Book Company we are dedicated to helping Christians and local churches grow. We believe that God's growth process always starts with hearing clearly what he has said to us through his timeless and flawless word—the Bible.

Ever since we opened our doors in 1991, we have been striving to produce resources that are biblical, relevant, and accessible. By God's grace, we have grown to become an international publisher, encouraging ordinary Christians of every age and stage and every background and denomination to live for Christ day by day and equipping churches to grow in their knowledge of God, their love for one another, and the effectiveness of their outreach.

Call one of our friendly team for a discussion of your needs or visit one of our local websites for more information on the resources and services we provide.

Your friends at The Good Book Company

thegoodbook.com | thegoodbook.co.uk
thegoodbook.com.au | thegoodbook.co.nz
thegoodbook.co.in